# NAPOLEON'S MARSHALS

*Napoleon with Davout on his right, Berthier and Murat on his left. Detail from the painting 'Napoleon in Berlin' by Berthon.*

# NAPOLEON'S MARSHALS

## Brigadier Peter Young

### D.S.O., M.C.

Colour plates by Michael Youens

OSPREY

First published in 1973 by
Osprey Publishing Limited
707 Oxford Road, Reading, Berkshire RG3 1JB

SBN 85045 112 4

Design: David Scurfield

Filmset and printed by BAS Printers Limited, Wallop, Hampshire

# Acknowledgements

I wish to express my grateful thanks to a number of friends who have helped me with the picture research for this book. They are W. Y. Carman, Marcus Hinton, Edward Surén, Roy Belmont-Maitland, and Arthur Johnston. The generous way in which they promptly assisted me with material from their collections has placed me very much in their debt.

The illustrations on pages 46, 67, 70, 89, 93, 99, 115, 121, 131, 135, 159, 165, 171, 175 and 187 come from the Museum of Versailles; on pages 53, 143, and 145 from the Mansell Collection; on page 45 from the Louvre; on page 35 from the Museum Châlon-sur-Saône; on page 29 from the collection of the Prince of Wagram; on page 155 from the collection of M. Rotham; on page 183 from the collection of Prince Poniatowski; on page 118 from the Parker Gallery; on page 105 from George Clinton Genet; on page 77 from the collection of M. Léon Lefebvre.

ERRATUM

The captions on pages 161 and 176 have become transposed. Page 161 should read EMMANUEL, MARQUIS DE GROUCHY. Page 176 should read PRINCE JOSEF ANTON PONIATOWSKI.

# Contents

List of Illustrations                                                    11
Introduction                                                             15
Annals of the Marshals                                                   19

1     Berthier                                                           27
2     Murat                                                              34
3     Moncey                                                             44
4     Jourdan                                                            51
5     Masséna                                                            55
6     Augereau                                                           66
7     Bernadotte                                                         71
8     Soult                                                              76
9     Brune                                                              87
10    Lannes                                                             91
11    Mortier                                                            98
12    Ney                                                               104
13    Davout                                                            120
14    Bessières                                                         127
15    Kellermann                                                        134
16    Lefebvre                                                          137
17    Pérignon                                                          141
18    Sérurier                                                          144
19    Victor                                                            148
20    Macdonald                                                         153
21    Oudinot                                                           157
22    Marmont                                                           163
23    Suchet                                                            169
24    Gouvion-Saint-Cyr                                                 174
25    Poniatowski                                                       181
26    Grouchy                                                           186

Notes on the Text                                                       192
Notes on the Colour Plates                                              195

Appendix 1: Napoleonic Generals made Marshals                           199
Appendix 2: Battles of the Revolution and Empire after 1815            201
Select bibliography                                                     203

# Illustrations

Napoleon with Davout, Berthier and Murat  *frontispiece*
Berthier  29
Murat  35
Berthier and Murat at the battle of Jena  43
Moncey at the barrière de Clichy  45
Moncey  46
Jourdan  53
Masséna  57
Masséna with his son Prosper and General Fririon  62
Augereau  67
Bernadotte  70
Soult  77
Soult in the uniform of Colonel-General of the
    Imperial Guard  84
Brune  89
Lannes  93
Napoleon visits Lannes after the battle of Essling  95
Mortier  99
Ney  105
Ney with his staff  108
Ney sustaining the rear-guard of the French Army  115
The execution of Ney  118
Davout  121
Bessières  131
Kellermann  135
Lefebvre  139
Pérignon  143
Sérurier  145
Victor  149
Macdonald  155
Oudinot  159
Marmont  165
Suchet  171
Gouvion-Saint-Cyr  175
Poniatowski  183
Grouchy  187
The Abdication  190

## COLOUR PLATES

Berthier and Guide                          *opposite page*   32
Murat and Officier d'Ordonnance, 1809                      33
Moncey and Éclaireur-Guide                                 48
Masséna                                                    49
Bernadotte                                                 80
Aide-de-camp and Guide of Bernadotte                       81
Lannes                                                     96
Suchet                                                     97
Ney                                                       112
Mortier and Guide                                         113
Bessières                                                 128
Davout                                                    129
Marmont                                                   160
Poniatowski                                               161
Grouchy                                                   176
Aide-de-camp of Berthier and Officier d'Ordonnance
    of Murat, 1812                                        177

CREEVEY: Do you calculate upon any desertion in Bonaparte's army?

WELLINGTON: Not upon a man from the colonel to the private in a regiment—both inclusive. We may pick up a marshal or two, perhaps; but not worth a damn.

*Conversation on about 4 June 1815*

# Introduction

In this book the careers of the Marshals are given in order of the date of their promotion: that is to say, the 18 Marshals of 1804 come first, including the four honorary Marshals, Kellermann, Lefebvre, Pérignon and Sérurier, despite the fact that they were always classed apart and below the active Marshals, even those promoted in later years.

It may be worth mentioning, *en passant*, that General Jean-Andoche Junot, Duc d'Abrantès (1771–1813), often said to have been a Marshal, was not so. Had he succeeded in defeating Lt.-General Sir Arthur Wellesley, K.B., at Vimeiro things might have been different.

At the head of each Marshal's career I have given his name and his French titles in French; elsewhere I have generally followed English usage. But not everything translates well into English. Is it really helpful to translate '*Maréchal des Logis*' into 'Sergeant-Major', or '*Chef de Brigade*' into 'Colonel'? I think not. Equally Murat's last words seem to me better left in the original. The *mots* with which Gallic soldiers have adorned the history of their Army lose most of their spirit when rendered into English. Again the names of French units often lose something by translation; my decision, therefore, to resist the temptation to translate '*Carabiniers de Monsieur*' or '*Volontaires du Nord*' will not, I trust, be found too arbitrary.

There are at least two popular and well-written works in English which deal with the careers of the Marshals. If they have a fault it is that they exaggerate the Marshals' bad qualities: their avarice, their quarrels, their ingratitude to the Emperor. They also seem somewhat uncritical in their use of sources, leaning rather too heavily on the more sensational memoirists of the period. Thanks to the works of Georges Six and Le Barrois d'Orgeval the careers of the Marshals may be traced with some precision, and it has seemed worth while to attempt to do so.

Part of the art of generalship lies in the field of Personnel Selection: in the choice of the best subordinates for great trusts. It is worth considering whether Napoleon's choice of Marshals is evidence of his skill in this respect. Were they great generals?

Kellermann, Jourdan and Masséna had great victories to their credit in the Revolutionary Wars, but of the three only the last seems to have been of outstanding merit. Berthier was purely a staff officer; Murat and Bessières were excellent cavalry officers but nothing more. Grouchy too should be classed with them, for he was primarily a cavalryman.

The best all-round soldiers of the twenty-six seem to have been Masséna, Davout, Soult, Suchet, Macdonald, Gouvion-Saint-Cyr and Marmont for in addition to their skill in strategy and tactics they were all good administrators. Unfortunately the last two, and especially Marmont, had defects of character which would make one hesitate to employ them. It may be that Brune, though not *persona grata* with the Emperor, was as good as some of these, though he was not employed so often.

Augereau, Lannes, Mortier, Ney, Lefebvre, Oudinot and Poniatowski were all good fighting soldiers at the corps level. Of this group Lannes and Ney were probably the best, but the former died too young for his true worth to be estimated, while Ney, perhaps owing to the hardships he endured in Russia, became somewhat unpredictable in his last campaigns.

Sérurier was an adequate divisional commander in Italy (1796), and both Moncey and Pérignon had good records during the Revolutionary Wars. Neither Bernadotte nor Victor seems to have merited his promotion.

It is easy to point to the Marshals' defects of character: the avarice of Soult and Masséna; the ingratitude of Berthier, Murat and Marmont; the cold selfishness of Gouvion Saint-Cyr. Moncey and Macdonald, on the other hand, were men of the highest character. Davout, if somewhat forbidding, steered a straight course, while Mortier was liked by friend and foe.

On the whole, Napoleon's selection, governed as it was to some extent by political considerations, was sound enough. True, by loading them with honours and riches he deprived some of his high officers of their desire for combat, but that is another matter.

One wonders why others, including Drouet and Gérard, who both received their batons under the restored Bourbons, were not promoted under the Empire. Had things gone differently on 18 June 1815 they would no doubt have been promoted sooner.

One last point is perhaps worth making. The nature of soldiers has changed very little over the years. It may be that nowadays in the selection of officers for high rank more emphasis is put on skill in staff work than on physical courage or even battle experience. But it seems to me that a study of the careers of Napoleon's Marshals still has a great deal to tell us about the military mind and the behaviour of soldiers under the stresses and strains of war – and peace.

There have been Marshals of France since the year 1047 – more than three hundred and thirty great soldiers, and in the words of Jean Brunon, who has done so much to preserve the traditions of the French Army: 'The history of the marshalate of France is the history of France herself in its most noble aspect.'

But there is one decided break in this long history, a break of nine years: 1793–1804. At the time of the execution of Louis XVI there were eight Marshals of France, created under the Old Régime. A month later, on 21 February 1793, the rank of Marshal was suppressed by the Assembly of the National Convention. Three Marshals perished on the guillotine and only one, Rochambeau, who had distinguished himself during the War of American Independence, lived to see the marshalate revived.

In 1804 the Emperor Napoleon created eighteen new Marshals, men who had fought their way to the fore thanks to their own talents and courage during the Revolutionary Wars: men from every class of society, all of whom had been in the Army before the *Levée en Masse* of 23 August 1793. Napoleon added to this number from time to time and in all twenty-six officers became Marshals under the Empire, though there were never more than twenty-one at any given time. Many of these men remained in the Army after the Restoration of 1815, and a number of generals who had served under

Napoleon became Marshals after his fall.* But in this book we are dealing only with that group of twenty-six actually promoted by the Emperor.

Since the career of many of the Marshals would fill a tome many times the size of this book, all are given here only in outline.

Even so it is well to remember that the oldest of them, Kellermann, was born in 1735, when Louis XV was on the throne of France, and that the last to die, Marmont, survived until 1852. Their lives span 117 years of the history of France, a period which saw her greatest military triumphs.

Where appropriate, Napoleon is also referred to as Buonaparte (up to 1796) and Bonaparte (1796 to 1804); and Wellington is also referred to as the Hon. Arthur Wesley (until 1798) and Sir Arthur Wellesley (1798 to 1809).

*See Appendix 1.

# Annals of the Marshals

| | |
|---|---|
| 1735 | Birth of Kellermann. |
| 1740–1748 | The War of the Austrian Succession. |
| 1742 | Birth of Sérurier. |
| 1747 | Marshal de Saxe becomes Maréchal-Général des Camps et Armées de France. |
| 1752 | Kellermann joins the army. |
| 1753 | Birth of Berthier. |
| 1754 | Pérignon and Moncey born. |
| 1755 | Birth of Lefebvre. Sérurier is commissioned. |
| 1756–1763 | The Seven Years War. |
| 1757 | Birth of Augereau. |
| 1758 | Birth of Masséna. |
| 1762 | Birth of Jourdan. |
| 1763 | Bernadotte, Poniatowski and Brune born. |
| 1764 | Gouvion Saint-Cyr and Victor born. |
| 1765 | Birth of Macdonald. |
| 1766 | Birth of Grouchy. Berthier joins the army. |
| 1767 | Murat and Oudinot born. |
| 1768 | Mortier and Bessières born. |
| 1769 | Ney, Soult and Lannes born—as well as Buonaparte and the Hon. Arthur Wesley. Moncey joins the Army. |
| 1770 | Suchet and Davout born. |
| 1773 | Lefebvre enlists. |
| 1774 | Augereau enlists. Birth of Marmont. |
| 1775 | Masséna enlists. |

1775–1783 The War of American Independence.

1778         Jourdan enrols.
Poniatowski commissioned in the Austrian Army.

1779         Jourdan serves at the Siege of Savannah.

1780         Grouchy, Pérignon and Bernadotte join the Army.

1781         Victor enlists.

1784         Oudinot and Macdonald[1] enlist.
Napoleon Buonaparte joins the Military School at Paris.

1785         Soult and Davout join the Army.
Napoleon Buonaparte joins the Artillery.

1787         Ney and Murat enlist.
Arthur Wesley commissioned in the British Army.

1789         The French Revolution breaks out.
Bessières, Brune and Mortier join the Army.

1790         Marmont commissioned.

1791         Suchet commissioned.

1792–1800 The French Revolutionary Wars.

1792         Gouvion-Saint-Cyr and Lannes enlist.
Battle of Valmy. Kellermann and Dumouriez defeat the Duke of Brunswick.

1793         King Louis XVI guillotined. (21 Jan.)
Suppression of the Marshalate. (21 Feb.)
The Reign of Terror. (July–August)
Battle of Wattignies. Jourdan defeats Saxe-Coburg.

1794         Marshals Count Luckner, the Duke de Mouchy and the Count de Mailly guillotined.
Siege of Toulon.
Battle of Fleurus. Jourdan defeats Saxe-Coburg.

1796         Bonaparte's Italian Campaign.
Battle of Castiglione. Augereau greatly distinguishes himself.

1797         Battle of Rivoli. Masséna plays a vital part.

1798–1801 French campaign in Egypt and Syria.

1799         Siege of Acre.
Battle of the Trebbia. Suvorov defeats Macdonald.
Battle of Abukir.
Bonaparte returns to France.
18 Brumaire.

1800 Masséna's defence of Genoa.
Lannes wins the battle of Montebello.
Battle of Marengo.

1802 Peace of Amiens ratified.

1803 Resumption of hostilities.

1804 Napoleon creates 18 Marshals (19 May).
Napoleon crowned Emperor.

1805 The first awards of the Grand Eagle of the Legion of Honour
(2 Feb.).
Ulm, Trafalgar and Austerlitz.

1806 Jena and Auerstädt.
Bernadotte made Prince of Pontecorvo.
Berthier Sovereign Prince of Neuchâtel and Valangin, and
Vice-Constable.
Murat made Grand-Duke of Berg and of Cleves.
Lefebvre created Duke of Danzig.

1807 Victor promoted Marshal.

1808 The Peninsular War.
Murat made King of Naples.
Ten Marshals are made dukes, and two, Pérignon and
Sérurier, are made counts.
Bessières defeats Cuesta at Medina del Rio Seco.

1809 Battle of Corunna between Soult and Sir John Moore.
Bessières made Duke of Istria.
Battle of Essling: Lannes mortally wounded, aged 40.
Battle of Wagram.
Masséna created Prince of Essling.
Macdonald, Count Oudinot and Marmont[2] promoted
Marshal.
Battle of Talavera.
Davout created Prince of Eckmühl.
Macdonald made Duke of Tarentum.

1810 Battle of Busaco. Wellington repulses Masséna.
Masséna is foiled by the Lines of Torres Vedras protecting
Lisbon.

1811 Battle of Fuentes de Oñoro. Wellington foils Masséna.
Suchet promoted Marshal.
Beresford defeats Soult at Albuera.

1812  Suchet is made Duke of Albufera.
     Wellington defeats Marmont at Salamanca.
     Gouvion-Saint-Cyr is promoted Marshal.

1813  Ney is made Prince of the Moskwa.
     Bessières killed on the eve of the battle of Lutzen, aged 44.
     Battle of Vitoria.
     Battle of the Pyrenees. Wellington repulses Soult.
     The Battle of Leipzig.
     Prince Poniatowski is promoted Marshal, but drowned three
       days later, aged 50.
     Battle of the Nivelle. Wellington defeats Soult.

1814  The campaign of France.
     Battle of Orthez. Wellington defeats Soult.
     Napoleon abdicates and is sent to Elba.
     Battle of Toulouse. Wellington drives Soult out of the city.

1815  Napoleon returns from Elba.
     Grouchy promoted Marshal.
     Berthier commits suicide—or is murdered.
     Brune made count.
     The campaign of Waterloo. Soult, Ney and Grouchy take
       part.
     Grouchy dismissed from the marshalate.
     Brune assassinated, aged 62.
     Moncey deprived of his rank and imprisoned.
     Davout exiled to Louviers.
     Augereau disgraced.
     Murat shot, aged 48.
     Ney shot, aged 46.

1816  Death of Augereau, aged 59.
     Soult exiled.
     Moncey reinstated.

1817  Death of Masséna, aged 59.
     Davout reinstated.

1818  Death of Pérignon, aged 64.

1819  Death of Sérurier, aged 77.
     Soult returns from exile.

1820  Deaths of Kellermann, aged 85, and Lefebvre, aged 74.

1821  Death of the Emperor Napoleon.

1823  Death of Davout, aged 53.

1826  Death of Suchet, aged 55.

1830    Death of Gouvion-Saint-Cyr, aged 65.
        Marmont struck from the list and exiled.

1833    Death of Jourdan, aged 71.

1835    Mortier killed by Fieschi's infernal machine, aged 67.

1840    Death of Macdonald, aged 74.
        Napoleon's body brought to the Invalides. Soult, Moncey,
            Oudinot and Grouchy present.

1841    Death of Victor, aged 76.

1842    Death of Moncey, aged 87.

1844    Death of Bernadotte, aged 81.

1847    Deaths of Grouchy and Oudinot, both at the age of 80.
        Soult made Marshal-General.

1851    Death of Soult, aged 82.

1852    Death of Marmont, aged 77.

# The Careers
# of the Marshals

I

# LOUIS-ALEXANDRE BERTHIER, PRINCE DE NEUCHÂTEL ET VALANGIN, PRINCE DE WAGRAM

## 1753–1815

> The Emperor's Wife.
> *soldiers' nickname*

For eighteen years Berthier was Napoleon Bonaparte's closest associate. He was his Chief of Staff in all his wars from Italy (1796) to the Campaign of France (1814). His absence from the Head-quarters of the Army of the North was sadly felt in 1815.

Under the Consulate and Empire, Berthier became something of a general factotum: Minister of War (1799–1807); Grand Hunts-man (1804); Vice-Constable (1807). Napoleon showered wealth upon him – he had by 1809 over a million francs a year – and made him a sovereign prince. He was honoured with orders and decorations by a dozen European sovereigns, including the rulers of France, Italy, Bavaria, Württemberg, Saxony, Baden, Hesse, Würzburg, Hungary, Prussia, Russia and Westphalia. He married the daughter of Prince William, the cousin and brother-in-law of the King of Württemberg.

The man who was thus loaded with wealth and honours was very far from being one of the great soldiers of all time. He was quite incapable of commanding an army, as he proved conclusively in the opening stages of the 1809 campaign when he commanded the Grand Army and managed to get it hopelessly scattered, with seventy-five miles between its wings and only a thin screen of Bavarians between. A note of 16 April reveals the depths of his anxiety and despair: 'In this position of affairs, I greatly desire the arrival of your Majesty, in order to avoid the orders and counter-orders which circumstances as well as the directives and instructions of your Majesty necessarily entail.' But if he did not understand how to manœuvre an army it was not for lack of battle experience. He was wounded in the arm by a musket ball at Marengo and by a lance-thrust in the head at Brienne.

Berthier's military talents lay entirely in the field of staff work and there he was unrivalled in his day. By modern standards the staff work of the Grand Army left much to be desired. The duties of the various departments were not clearly defined and this led to duplication of effort. Moreover the entire organization was top-heavy and cumbersome. But for this Napoleon rather than Berthier must bear the blame, for the Emperor was a chronic over-centralizer. He relied on his staff to provide information and to transmit his orders; he did not expect it to do his planning. Hence the oft-repeated gibe that Berthier was little more than his chief clerk. In criticizing these pioneers of staff work it is worth considering that their system was vastly superior to that of the Army they inherited, and to those of the armies they opposed. Of their contemporaries only Wellington, with his practical common sense, succeeded in devising a truly efficient and comprehensive method of running all the departments of an army. And, of course, the British Army in the Peninsula was a much smaller concern than the Grand Army.

Berthier, born at Versailles on 20 November 1753, was fifteen years older than Napoleon and had joined the Army of the Old Régime as an *ingénieur géographe* on 1 January 1766. He had served both in the dragoons and in the infantry and had been on Rochambeau's staff in America (1781). When the Revolution broke out he was already a lieutenant-colonel and a chevalier of Saint-Louis.

Between 1791 and 1792 he served on Rochambeau's staff. Then he was Chief of Staff, first to La Fayette, then to Luckner. At the height of the Terror he was suspended from his functions (20

BERTHIER
*From the painting by Antoine-Jean Gros, engraved by H. Davidson.*

September 1792), and it was not until 5 March 1795 that he was reinstated, with the rank of General of Brigade, and made Chief of Staff of the Army of the Alps and of Italy. He was already a General of Division (promoted 13 June 1795) before Bonaparte arrived. Thereafter they served together until the first abdication with only a few days' separation. But these few days were significant, for during the first of them in 1809 Berthier had his opportunity to demonstrate his total incapacity for high command. And the second spell was when Napoleon quit the Grand Army at Smorgonie (1812) leaving his Chief of Staff to serve the King of Naples, an arrangement which did not please Berthier in the least. He had hoped for a place in the Emperor's sleigh.

Berthier has been described as 'small, stout, ever laughing, very full of business'. But, despite rank and riches, it was no joke serving Napoleon Bonaparte. When the latter's ambitions took him to Egypt Berthier missed his adored Madame Giuseppina Visconti. When Napoleon shot Masséna in the eye the Grand Huntsman had to take the blame. By 1812 he was complaining: 'I am being killed by hard work. A mere soldier is happier than I!' No wonder he bit his nails!

By the end of the Campaign of France, Berthier, like most of his fellow Marshals, had become thoroughly disillusioned by interminable campaigning. He was among the first to abandon the Emperor. He accepted the Bourbons who made him Captain of the 5th Company of the Gardes du Corps (1 June 1814), a Peer of France (4 June) and a commander of Saint-Louis (25 September).

When Napoleon returned from Elba, Berthier escorted King Louis XVIII to Ghent, but then went to Bamberg in Bavaria, where he died in mysterious circumstances on 1 June 1815. Some say that he was murdered by six masked men, others that, seeing Allied troops on the march towards France, he hurled himself from a window in a fit of remorse. The latter story seems the more likely.

Napoleon was genuinely fond of his Chief of Staff. On his defection in 1814 he exclaimed: 'Berthier's desertion has broken my heart! My old friends, my comrades in arms!' And when on 5 June 1815 he heard of the Marshal's death he fainted, it is said, from emotion. The fact is that Berthier, a born worrier, had not the back-bone to stand up to the stresses and strains of the terrible campaigns of 1812–14. At the end of the road Napoleon described his old comrade as 'véritable oison, que j'avais fait une espèce d'aigle'. It was unkind perhaps, but not inaccurate.

Berthier had two younger brothers, both of whom served in the Artillery Regiment of La Fère under the Old Régime and became Generals of Division under the Empire. They were Louis-César-Gabriel, dit de Berluy, Comte Berthier (1765–1819) and Victor-Léopold Berthier (1770–1807). They were both staff officers rather than fighting men.

LOUIS-ALEXANDRE BERTHIER,
Prince de Neuchâtel et Valangin, Prince de Wagram  (left)

(right) Guide de Berthier

································································································

## JOACHIM, PRINCE MURAT,
Grand-Duc de Berg et de Clèves, Roi de Naples (left)

································································································

(right) Officier d'Ordonnance de Murat, 1809

# JOACHIM, PRINCE MURAT, GRAND-DUC DE BERG ET DE CLÈVES, ROI DE NAPLES

## 1767–1815

It would be better if he was endowed with rather less courage and rather more common sense.

GENERAL SAVARY[1]

*10 June 1807*

On 4 October 1793 *chef d'escadrons* Murat of the 16th Chasseurs brought forty guns from the Plain of Sablons to the Tuileries, the guns from whose mouths General Buonaparte discharged the 'whiff of grapeshot' of the 13 Vendémiaire. On 20 January 1800 the First Consul gave his sister Caroline in marriage to General of Division Murat, the commander of the Consular Guard. On 19 May 1804 the name of General Murat, Governor of Paris, was second on the list of the eighteen newly created Marshals of the Empire.

To say that his military talents demanded that Murat be of this number would be the gravest exaggeration. Which is not to say that the handsome, volatile Gascon was altogether lacking in the military virtues. In an army of brave men his courage and dash were exceptional. He had the gift of inspiring cavalry to follow him on the day of battle – though he was scarcely the ablest of Napoleon's great cavalry generals. As a commander of an army or of a corps of all arms he was at best indifferent. Loaded with honours, he lacked the moral character to follow any path other than that of self-interested ambition. In his ostentatious love of extravagant military

MURAT
*From the crayon drawing by François Gérard, engraved by Henry Wolf.*

costumes there was something of the buffoon – indeed he was deeply hurt on one occasion when Napoleon compared him to Signor Franconi the well-known circus rider. The description must have given malicious pleasure to the hot-tempered Murat's many enemies.

Murat was born the son of an innkeeper, at La Bastide-Fortunière[2] (Lot) on 25 March 1767. He was educated at the seminary of Cahors, and went on to study theology at Toulouse. He got himself expelled from the seminary and on his return home was ill-received by his family. So on 23 February 1787 he enlisted as a trooper in the Chasseurs des Ardennes.[3] From 8 February to 4 March 1792

35

he was in the Constitutional Guard of Louis XVI, and when that body was dismissed, he went back to the 12th Chasseurs.

29 April 1792:      *Brigadier* (corporal)
15 May 1792:        *Maréchal des Logis*
15 October 1792:    *Sous-Lieutenant*
31 October 1792:    *Lieutenant*

In 1792 and 1793 he served in Champagne and with the Army of the North. The brave General Auguste-Marie-Henri Picot, Marquis de Dampierre (1756–93) made him provisional A.D.C. to General Joseph-François-Jean-Baptiste d'Urre de Molans (1743–1817), who had been a captain in the Bercheny Hussars under the Old Régime. Dampierre provisionally made him *chef d'escadrons* in the 16th Chasseurs (May 1793).

At this period his political views were extreme. He wanted to change his name to Marat when the latter was assassinated! After the 9 Thermidor he was denounced, but, though he lost his rank and was unemployed for a time, the Committee of Public Safety annulled the accusation. It was at this juncture that the Sablons incident put him on the path to a crown – and the firing squad. Without Murat's energy the guns would have been in the wrong hands and there would have been no 'whiff of grapeshot' on the 13 Vendémiaire (5 October).

Murat had to wait some time for his reward, but as soon as Bonaparte was given command of the Army of Italy he made him his chief A.D.C. (29 February 1796). On 2 February Murat had been promoted *chef de brigade* with effect from 18 November 1793.

Murat served at Dego, Ceva and Mondovi and was sent to Paris with the colours taken from the enemy. On 10 May he was promoted General of Brigade, commanded the cavalry at Borghetto (30 May), and then commanded a cavalry brigade on the River Adige (10 July). On 12 September he was wounded at San Giorgio. He was given command (20 December) of the cavalry of the division of General Gabriel-Venance Rey (1763–1836) and commanded his advanced guard. Rey was sent to France in charge of a column of 20,000 Austrian prisoners (21 January 1797) and Murat found himself commanding the division, and served under Joubert in the Tirol. He served at the battle of the Tagliamento (16 March). During the months that followed he commanded several different formations including a light infantry brigade (14 June–5 August 1797).

Murat went to Egypt in command of a brigade of dragoons. He distinguished himself at the capture of Alexandria, fought at the Pyramids and commanded the cavalry in the Syrian expedition. He led a good charge at Abukir and was severely wounded, his jaw being shattered by a pistol shot. He found himself lying in hospital with his face swathed in bandages. In the next bed was his fellow Gascon, Lannes, who detested him and had not been deprived of the power of speech. It must have been an uneasy convalescence. Still Bonaparte had made him General of Division on the field of battle – which was some consolation.

Murat was one of the fortunate band selected to return to France with Bonaparte, and on the 18 Brumaire it was he who sent sixty grenadiers into the Orangery to eject the deputies, a stroke which won him command of the Consular Guard (2 December 1799). In the following January he was married to Caroline Bonaparte.

In the 1800 campaign Murat commanded the cavalry of the Army of Reserve, and won a sabre of honour by his bravery at Marengo. He was soon back in France and commanding a corps of grenadiers encamped between Beauvais and Amiens (1 August). His next command (27 November) was an observation corps concentrated at Dijon and directed against central Italy. He occupied Tuscany and chased the Neapolitans from the Papal States, signing the Armistice of Foligno (6 February 1801) with the King of Naples. He seized the Isle of Elba and laid siege to Portoferraio.

On 15 January 1804 Murat became Governor of Paris; it was he who convened the court that condemned the Duc d'Enghien to be shot. In 1804 he was promoted Marshal of the Empire. Further honours followed on 1 February 1805 when he was made Grand Admiral and Prince. On the day following he was invested with the Grand Eagle of the Legion of Honour.

In the 1805 campaign he commanded the Reserve Cavalry of the

Grand Army, which with the light cavalry brigades of Napoleon's various corps maintained an impenetrable screen between the French and Austrian armies. He and Lannes, in the first sharp action of the campaign on 8 October, virtually destroyed a small Austrian force at Wertingen, taking 2,000 prisoners. The Emperor, with his centre of operations at Augsburg, and his corps disposed against every eventuality, added two of them to Murat's command and put him temporarily in charge of the forces moving in on Mack at Ulm. Napoleon estimated that the Austrians were 40,000 strong and would fight: 'It is therefore imperative', he wrote (11 October), 'that your reserve and the corps of Ney and Lannes, which together make some 50,000–60,000 men, should march as closely together as possible, so as to be able to reunite within the space of six hours in order to crush the enemy.'

Murat, believing that Mack's whole force was south of the Danube, had already ordered Ney to move two of his three divisions to the south bank. Ney had remonstrated on the morning of 11 October, only to receive from Murat a public and senseless rebuff: 'I know nothing of plans except those made in the presence of the enemy,' adding another to the list of his deadly enemies, and earning the first of a series of crushing rebukes from the Emperor. For Murat's manœuvres had left Dupont's[4] Division (Ney's Corps), 4,000 strong, exposed to battle with the Archduke Ferdinand and a force of 25,000 Austrians, which included 10,000 cavalry. It was no thanks to Prince Murat that Dupont, after holding out all day, managed to withdraw successfully. During the week that followed Murat made some amends by a relentless pursuit and the capture of large numbers of men, guns and vehicles.

Napoleon now planned to trap the wily old General Kutuzov. Murat had a sharp action with him at Amstetten (5 November), but, deceived as to the whereabouts and intentions of the enemy's main body, pressed on and entered Vienna (13 November), allowing Kutuzov not only to escape but to fall upon Mortier's corps isolated at Dürrenstein (10–11 November). This brought down upon Murat's head one of the best 'rockets' ever discharged by his imperial brother-in-law: 'I cannot approve of your method of operating; you proceed like a bewildered idiot, taking not the least notice of my orders.' The Prince now had the extraordinary good luck to bluff the Austrians into surrendering a vital bridge at Vienna, and the Emperor readily forgave his previous follies.

Murat served at Austerlitz, and at the end of the campaign was handsomely rewarded, being made Grand Dignitary of the Order of the *Couronne de Fer* (20 February 1806) and Grand-Duke of Berg and Cleves (15 March). He was now a sovereign prince, ruling over territories with which Prussia had vainly attempted to buy Napoleon's friendship. For this step upwards Murat had to thank his wife's campaigning against her brother, rather than his own against the Austrians and Russians. Caroline Murat was nothing if not persistent in her quest for social advancement.

Murat served at Jena and played a leading part in the pursuit that followed. He took 9,000–14,000 prisoners at Erfurt (15 October). At Prenzlau he succeeded in convincing Prince Friedrich Ludwig von Hohenlohe that he was surrounded by 100,000 Frenchmen. The Prussian surrendered with 10,000 men and 64 guns (28 October). On 28 November Murat entered Warsaw.

After a minor success at Hoff (6 February) Murat played an important role in the battle of Eylau, the first great check to the Grand Army. At the crisis of the battle, when the shattered French centre was in peril, he led a charge of 80 squadrons, 10,700 men,[5] which swept forward for 2,500 yards, crashed through the Russian centre, sabred their gunners by the score, and charged back again. For the loss of 1,500 men he had won time for Davout to come up, had taken the pressure off the Grand Army and given it new heart. It was by far his greatest military exploit, and one of the greatest cavalry charges in history.

At the battle of Heilsberg Murat was routed by Prince Bagration and General Uvarov, and his cavalry were only saved by the timely arrival of General Savary with the Fusiliers of the Guard and twelve guns. So far from thanking Savary Murat reviled him for cowardice! Recriminations followed the crude frontal attack at Heilsberg, and though Napoleon silenced the outspoken comments of Savary and Lannes, he did not forget what they had to say of Murat's behaviour.

On 16 June Murat took Königsberg, and was not therefore at Friedland on the 14th. The pursuit after that battle was a feeble affair, and Murat's worst enemies were compelled to admit that things would have been different had he been present. A shower of decorations now came his way from Würzburg, Saxony and, somewhat surprisingly, from Prussia and Russia. One can scarcely imagine Frederick the Great awarding the Black Eagle to a victorious enemy.

Murat was made Lieutenant of the Emperor in Spain (20 February 1808), and on 24 March he entered Madrid amidst cheering crowds. But when on 2 May (the *Dos de Mayo*) the mob rose, Murat suppressed the insurrection with a heavy hand, forfeiting his short-lived popularity. Soon after, on 15 June, he quitted the appointment owing to an attack of colic. In August Napoleon, having made his brother Joseph King of Spain and the Indies, decided to keep Naples and the Two Sicilies in the family and gave the crown to Murat. Spain was to be the graveyard of many Marshals' reputations, and Murat was lucky to leave it. One can scarcely imagine a *sabreur* of his sort coping successfully with a strategist of Wellington's calibre.

Proclaimed King of Naples on 1 August 1808, Murat indulged in some musical comedy campaigning of the kind that showed off his latest uniforms to the greatest advantage. He besieged Capri, compelling Lt.-Colonel Hudson Lowe[6] to capitulate. He failed in an expedition against Sicily in 1809.

The King of Naples commanded the Reserve Cavalry in the campaign of 1812. In fighting around Krasnoe on 15 August he lost his head and, despite Ney's pleas, delivered a series of piecemeal cavalry charges against the Russian squares, which succeeded only in preventing the 3rd Corps moving up into action. Just before Borodino he managed to fall out with Davout, who thought he was mismanaging his overworked cavalry. During the battle his men charged the Russian squares in vain, and all four of his corps commanders were hit. He supported the Emperor in his decision not to launch the Guard, though its intervention would probably have proved decisive after the fall of the Grand Redoubt. But by about 10 p.m. he had changed his mind, and appealed to Napoleon to let him use the cavalry of the Guard. Gorgeously apparelled, he was among the first to enter Moscow about midnight on 14 September.

Murat was surprised at Vinkovo on 18 October, but managed to fight his way out. The retreat from Moscow began next day. When the army reached Smorgonie Napoleon revealed his intention to depart. 'A vous, Roi de Naples!' said he (5 December) – perhaps the briefest handover of command in history. The King was shattered by what he had seen on the retreat. Instructed to give his men eight days' rest at Vilna, he ordered its evacuation on the 9th, leaving 20,000 wounded in the hospitals.

On 18 January 1813 Murat handed over command of the Grand Army and set off for the sunnier clime of Naples. For this Napoleon rebuked him very properly in Le Moniteur: 'The King of Naples, being indisposed, has been obliged to resign his command of the army, which he has handed over to the Prince Viceroy.[7] The latter is more accustomed to the management of important affairs.'

Murat now entered into secret negotiations with England and Austria with the object of retaining his throne, come what might. In the summer Napoleon, who had expected him to return and put his cavalry into some semblance of order, wrote: 'I presume you are not one of those who believe the lion to be dead ... if you make this calculation you are very much mistaken.' Thus prodded, the King rejoined the Grand Army in Saxony in August 1813, serving at Dresden, where he did rather well, and Leipzig, where he led his last great charge, though with very limited success.

Soon afterwards he left Napoleon for ever, returning to Naples 'to raise new troops' (5 November). Needless to say, they never materialized, for Murat lost no time in signing treaties with Austria and Great Britain (6 and 11 January 1814) by which he engaged to provide 30,000 men against France in return for a guarantee that he should retain his crown. Napoleon was understandably incensed. To Fouché he wrote: 'The conduct of the King of Naples is infamous, and that of the Queen quite unspeakable. I hope to live long enough to avenge myself and France for such an outrage and such horrible ingratitude.' Murat now seized Reggio and compelled Prince Eugène to quit the line of the River Adige.

Upon the return of the Bourbons Murat found his throne threatened, so upon Napoleon's return from Elba he assured him of his fidelity. Making Queen Caroline his regent he published a manifesto (30 March) calling upon the people of Italy to fight for their independence, and seized Florence with his army. Defeated at Tolentino (2 May), he escaped to France and offered his services to Napoleon, who did not deign to reply. From Fouché Murat received an order not to go to Paris. He was at Lyons when he heard the news of Waterloo, and went to Toulon where he learned that there was a price on his head. After days in hiding he reached Corsica, and mounted a desperate attempt to regain his kingdom – as Napoleon had done from Elba. Landing with only 30 men at Pizzo[8] in Calabria he was captured after a brief skirmish, court-martialled without delay on 13 October, condemned and half an hour later executed.

He made a good end. He refused to sit down, or to permit himself to be blindfolded. To the firing squad he said: 'Sauvez la tête, visez au cœur!'

Murat had struck great blows for the Emperor – notably at Eylau; but he had also dealt him mortal blows. When on the evening of 6 February 1814 Napoleon heard from the Viceroy of his defection he exclaimed: 'No, it cannot be! Murat, to whom I have given my sister! Murat, to whom I have given a throne! Eugène must be mistaken. It is impossible that Murat should have declared himself against me.' But when all is said and done, the Emperor had only himself to blame if he loaded honours and advancement on a brave hothead, who, though not altogether lacking in talent, lacked the character for great place.

*A detail from Thevenin's painting of the battle of Jena, executed for Berthier in 1810. Murat is on the left of the group; next to him is Berthier. The figure on the far right is one of Berthier's A.D.C.s.*

# BON-ADRIEN-JEANNOT DE MONCEY, DUC DE CONEGLIANO
## 1754–1842

Que tout le monde remplisse sa carrière comme j'ai rempli la mienne.[1]
MARSHAL MONCEY

Moncey was born at Moncey (Doubs) on 31 July 1754, the son of an advocate in the Parliament of Besançon. On 15 September 1769 he joined the *Champagne-infanterie* as a volunteer, but bought his discharge on 30 June 1773. On 8 April 1774 he became a soldier in the company of Gendarmes Anglais, which on 15 August 1776 he quitted 'par inconscience et légèreté. Jolie tournure, mais peu regrettable ; à ne pas reprendre', as the Roll of the Corps recorded. Despite this he became a *sous-lieutenant* in an infantry unit, *Nassau-Siegen* (16 August 1779) rising to the rank of *lieutenant en premier* before transferring to the 5th battalion of Chasseurs (1 June 1788). He was promoted captain (1 April 1791) and from 1793 to 1795 he served in the Pyrenees, seeing a good deal of fighting and gaining rapid promotion:

26 June 1793 :     *Chef de bataillon, 5ᵉ Demi-Brigade Légère.*

18 February 1794 :   General of Brigade (provisional).

9 June 1794 :     General of Division.

He defeated the Marquis de Saint-Simon at Arquinzun (9 July) and stormed the enemy entrenchments in the valley of Bastan with the bayonet (27, 28 and 30 July). He followed this up by seizing the port of Pasajes (2 August) and the city and citadel of San Sebastián, with 200 guns. He distinguished himself at the siege of Tolosa, and the Representatives of the People gave him provisional command

44

of the Army of the Pyrénées Occidentales, in which he was confirmed by the Committee of Public Safety (17 August 1794). In this appointment he met with considerable success, taking Bilbao on 19 July 1795.

After the *coup d'état* of Fructidor he was denounced as a Royalist, and until the end of November 1799 he was unemployed. In 1800 he held commands in Switzerland and Italy, and was at the passage of the Mincio at Monzembano (26 December). Brune intended to relieve him of his appointment for letting the enemy give him the slip, but in fact he retained it and commanded the Army of Italy in place of Brune from 8 March to 19 June 1801. After holding other commands in Italy he became senior inspector-general of gendarmerie (3 December 1801). He accompanied Bonaparte to

*Moncey at the barrière de Clichy, in the defence of Paris, 1814. From the painting by Horace Vernet, engraved by Peter Aitken.*

MONCEY
*From the painting by Jacques-Luc Barbier-Walbonne.*

the Low Countries in 1803, was made a Marshal on 19 May 1804 and invested with the Grand Eagle of the Legion of Honour in 1805.

On 16 December 1807 he was given command of the Corps of Observation of the Coasts of the Ocean, which he led to Spain (9 January 1808) and with which, after winning a victory at Los Capreras, he failed before Valencia.

Moncey was made Duke of Conegliano on 2 July 1808. He won minor victories at Almanza (3 July) and Lerin (3 October) where he commanded the 3rd Corps of the Army of Spain. He served under Lannes at Tudela (23 November) and for a time directed the siege of Saragossa.

He saw no fighting between 1809 and 1814, though he held high commands in Belgium and France. On 8 January 1814 he was made *major-général* of the National Guard of Paris, with whom he played a leading part in the defence of Paris, directing in person the gallant and tenacious resistance at the *barrière de Clichy* (30 March). After the capitulation he assembled the remnants of his force in the Champs-Elysées and led them to Fontainebleau.

King Louis XVIII retained him as inspector-general of gendarmerie and he was made a peer of France on 4 June 1814, and again by Napoleon during the Hundred Days (2 June 1815).

Marshal Moncey refused to preside over the court martial on Ney and for this was deprived of his rank and title (29 August) and condemned to three months in prison, which he served in the fortress of Ham. He was, however, restored to his rank and pay on 3 July 1816, and made a peer once more on 5 March 1819.

He took the field again in the Spanish campaign of 1823, when he beat the former guerrilla chief, Mina, and conquered Catalonia. He was given the Grand Cross of the Order of Saint-Louis on 9 October 1823. Moncey was made Governor of the Hôtel Royal des Invalides on 17 December 1833. He was a chevalier of *Saint-Esprit*, and of the *Couronne de Fer*; and also received the Grand Cross of the Order of Charles III of Spain, and the Grand Cordon of Saint Vladimir of Russia (1st Class).

Since Berthier and Murat were sovereign princes Moncey was

................................................

## BON-ADRIEN-JEANNOT DE MONCEY,
Duc de Conegliano (left)
................................................

(right) Éclaireur-Guide de Moncey

........................................................................................

## ANDRÉ MASSÉNA,
### Duc de Rivoli, Prince d'Essling

........................................................................................

*doyen* of the Marshals from 1809 to 1813 inclusive, and from 1 June 1815 (when Berthier died) until his death in 1842. Although he was temporarily deprived of his rank, his name did not disappear from the *Almanach Royal* of 1815/1816.

With the restoration of the monarchy the position of *doyen* of the Marshals recovered the importance it had enjoyed under the Old Régime. In those days the tribunal of the Marshals of France had sat normally at the residence of the senior Marshal, who enjoyed all the rights and honours of Constable.

# 4

# JEAN-BAPTISTE,
# COMTE JOURDAN
## 1762–1833

The Victor of Fleurus.

The victor of Wattignies and Fleurus won his place in history without the aid of Napoleon Bonaparte. Born at Limoges (Haute-Vienne) on 29 April 1762, Jourdan was the son of a surgeon – a profession which in those days had no great social status. He became a soldier at the *dépot des colonies* at the *Île de Ré* (2 April 1778) and, posted to the *régiment d'Auxerrois* (10 December), took part in the American War of Independence, being present at d'Estaing's unsuccessful siege of Savannah in September. He fell ill and returned to France (1 January 1782), where he rejoined his regiment (12 November 1783). Discharged on 26 July 1784, he set up as a mercer at Limoges and got married (22 January 1788), to a modiste. At the outbreak of the Revolution he became a captain in the National Guard of Limoges (July 1789), being, it seems, a sincere Republican. His advancement was rapid for on 9 October 1791 he was promoted lieutenant-colonel in the 2nd Battalion of Volunteers of Haute-Vienne. He was with the Army of the North during 1792 and 1793. He served at Jemappes (6 November 1792) and Neerwinden (18 March 1793), being promoted General of Brigade (27 May) and of Division (30 July). He fought at Linselles (18 August), where the Brigade of Guards made short work of his *sans-culottes*.

Jourdan commanded the French centre at the battle of Hondschoote (8 September) and was hit in the chest by a grapeshot. When General Jean-Nicolas Houchard (1738–1793[1]) was disgraced for his retreat from Menin, Jourdan was given command of the Army of the North in his place (22 September) and defeated Friedrich-Josias, Prince of Saxe-Coburg at Wattignies (15/16 October) only to be relieved of his command on 6 January 1794.

He was, however, soon back in harness, being made Commander-in-Chief of the Army of the Moselle on 10 March in place of Hoche. On 26 June he again defeated Saxe-Coburg at Fleurus. Then at the head of the newly created Army of the Sambre et Meuse, he entered Brussels and on 16 July took Namur. Though he saw a good deal of fighting in the next few years, he was not destined to reach these heights again. Indeed at Würzburg and Stockach he suffered defeat.

Jourdan was deputy for the Haute-Vienne in the Council of the Five Hundred and as such he opposed the *coup* of 18 Brumaire. He was expelled in consequence and even threatened with deportation, but his career was not long in jeopardy. His name was erased from the list of deportees (December 1799) and soon afterwards (21 January 1800) he was made inspector-general of infantry and cavalry. On 24 July he was made Ambassador to the Cisalpine Republic, and on 2 April 1801 Administrator-General of Piedmont. From 26 January 1804 to 6 September 1805 he was commander of the Army of Italy. He was made a Marshal of the Empire in 1804 and in 1805 he was decorated with the Grand Eagle of the Legion of Honour.

In 1806 Jourdan was Governor of Naples and Chief of Staff to King Joseph. When the Peninsular War broke out he was appointed Chief of Staff of the Army of Spain (17 July 1808), taking up the appointment on 22 August. He replaced Lefebvre as commander of the 4th Corps (10 January to 21 February 1809). He and Victor were repulsed by Wellesley at Talavera (28 July), but won a victory at Almonacid (11 August). He returned to France in October.

He was back in Spain as Governor of Madrid (8 July 1811), becoming, once more, Chief of Staff to King Joseph (16 March 1812). He was by no means incapable but his master was not the man to impose his will and Jourdan's plans on Marmont, Soult or Suchet. After Salamanca (22 July 1812) Wellington's star was in the ascendant and it was against Jourdan's advice that King Joseph fought at Vitoria (21 June 1813). As they rode away from that disastrous rout it is said that Jourdan remarked to the King: 'Well,

JOURDAN
*After a drawing by Ambrose Tardieu.*

Sire, you have had your battle – and it seems it was a defeat.' But if the Marshal blamed the King, the Emperor blamed the Marshal and he was recalled (12 July) and retired (7 August 1813).

Jourdan emerged once more as commander of the 14th and 15th Military Divisions at Rouen on 30 January 1814. In April he supported the provisional government, and was rewarded by being made a chevalier of Saint-Louis (2 June), and from 21 June 1814 to 27 September 1815 he was Governor of the 15th Military Division.

When Napoleon returned from Elba Jourdan, rather surprisingly, rallied to his cause, and was made a peer of France (2 June 1815), Governor of Besançon and commander of the 6th Military Division (4 June).

After Waterloo, Jourdan lost no time in changing sides yet again and he was President of the Council of War which condemned Marshal Ney. In 1816 King Louis XVIII made the old republican a Count and in 1825 gave him the Orders of Saint-Esprit and Saint-Michel. On 11 August 1830 he was made Governor of Les Invalides, where he ruled for three years over men who had been *sans-culottes* under him in his great days in 1793 and 1794, and not a few of whom, like him, had worn the King's white coat in the far-off days when d'Estaing had bungled his assault on Savannah.

# ANDRÉ MASSÉNA, DUC DE RIVOLI, PRINCE D'ESSLING
## 1758–1817

L'Enfant chéri de la Victoire.

GENERAL BONAPARTE
*After the battle of La Favorita*
*16 January 1797*

Masséna's titles derive respectively from an early triumph of General Bonaparte and a decided check to the Emperor Napoleon. But he had just titles of his own to his place in Valhalla: his victory at Zürich and his defence of Genoa. As a general he was cunning, tenacious and bold. As a human being his ruling passions were avarice and lechery. Above all he was a man of the world with a cynical understanding of human nature, rivalled by Talleyrand alone among contemporary Frenchmen.

This wily little man, with an Italian sort of good looks, was born at Nice on 6 May 1758 and went to sea in 1771 as a cabin boy in a ship trading in the Mediterranean and the Atlantic as far as Guiana.

He served in the old French regular army from 1775 to 1789 and was a useful N.C.O.

18 August 1775: Enlisted voluntarily in the *Régiment Royal-Italien*, later the battalion of Royal Chasseurs of Provence.

1 September 1776: Corporal, attached to the *peloton d'instruction*.

13 April 1777: Sergeant.

14 February 1783: *Fourrier* (quartermaster).

55

4 September 1784: *Adjudant sous-officier.*

3 August 1789: Discharged.

To have been promoted Sergeant at 19 years of age and after less than twenty months in the army of the Old Régime may surely be taken as proof, not only of literacy, but of great intelligence, diligence and aptitude.

Upon his discharge Masséna married a Mademoiselle Lamarre, the daughter of a surgeon, opened a dried fruit shop at Antibes, and is alleged to have used it as a front for a profitable smuggling business. He found little difficulty, it is said, in anticipating the counter-moves of the customs officials. However that may be, he can only have pursued this amusing and profitable vocation for about two years, for in 1791 he was made *adjudant-major*, first of the National Guard of Antibes, then (21 September) of the 2nd Battalion of Volunteers of the Var. His efficiency was quickly recognized and on 1 February 1792 he was elected lieutenant-colonel.

Masséna served with the Army of Italy from 1792 to 1798, being promoted General of Brigade (22 August 1793) and provisional General of Division (20 December) after his successful assaults on Forts Lartigue and Sainte-Catherine at Toulon (17 December 1793). On 29 August 1794 the Committee of Public Safety confirmed him in the rank of General of Division.

During 1794 and 1795 Masséna's career, like that of the army in which he served, had its ups and downs. On 22 December 1794 he had to give up his command because of sickness. When he recovered in the following April he took command of the 1st Division of the right wing of the Army. Repulsed by the Austrians at Melogno (25 June), he failed again at the attack on the redoubt there (27 June). He won the battle of Loano (23–25 November). Then Bonaparte arrived. In March 1796 there was an interview at Nice between the new General-in-Chief and his divisional commanders, who included three future marshals, Masséna, Augereau and Sérurier. All three were a bit fed up with an uphill struggle waged with a half-starved rabble of shoeless, ragged, ill-disciplined *sans-culottes.* They were all older men and older soldiers than this little Corsican, and when he came into the room they did not so much as

MASSÉNA
*From a lithograph by Delpech.*

deign to uncover. General Bonaparte took off his hat, obliging them
to do so too. No sooner had they doffed their plumed hats than he
clapped his own on his head again and stared them in the eye. They
lowered their gaze. Then he gave them his orders: polite, but curt
and unequivocal. Once outside, the veterans looked at each other
uneasily. Masséna, who knew more about people than the two others
put together, spoke for all: 'That little scoundrel only just missed
frightening me.' It had been a salutary experience, it seems, for
Masséna now began to display the most remarkable form. That not
only for Bonaparte was 1796 an *annus mirabilis* is revealed by this
bare summary of Masséna's fighting record:

| | |
|---|---|
| 12 April: | Combat of Montenotte. |
| 14/15 April: | Dego. |

57

| 25 April: | Takes Cherasco. |
| 10 May: | Storms the bridge of Lodi. |
| | The first to enter Milan. |
| 3 June: | Occupies Verona. |
| 3 August: | Victor at Lonato. |
| 5 August: | Battle of Castiglione. |
| 6 August: | Relieves Peschiera. |
| 8 September: | Serves at Bassano. |
| 14 September: | Repulsed at Due Castelli. |
| 15 September: | Serves at San Giorgio. |
| 8 November: | Serves on the Brenta. |
| 12 November: | Serves at Caldiero. |
| 15–17 November: | Battle of Arcola. |

1797

| 12 January: | Victor at San Michele. |
| 14 January: | Plays a leading rôle in the battle of Rivoli |
| 16 January: | and at La Favorita. |
| 19 March: | Seizes the Fort de la Chiusa |
| 22 March: | and the pass of Tarvis. |
| 2 April: | Victor at Neumarkt |
| 3 April: | and at Unzmarkt. |

It was a whirlwind! Bonaparte selected Masséna to present the preliminaries of Leoben to the Directory.

The next two years were comparatively peaceful and although Masséna continued in high command it was not until 9 April 1799, when he assumed command of the armies of the Danube and of Helvetia in Jourdan's stead, that he had a task worthy of his mettle. It fell to him to oppose the three-pronged Russo-Austrian invasion of Switzerland, with that eccentric Russian genius, General Suvorov, fighting his way across the Saint-Gotthard. Masséna's great victory at Zürich (25/26 September 1799) compelled the Allies to make a disastrous retreat. Had he not done so, Bonaparte might well have returned from Egypt to find the Russian, Austrian and British armies in France fifteen years before they actually got there!

Masséna's next command was the Army of Italy. He set up his

Headquarters at Nice on 17 January 1800, and then moved to Genoa, where he was shut up by the Austrians (5 April). He held out with tenacity and taught his men to subsist on loaves baked from sawdust, starch, hair-powder, linseed, cocoa, rancid nuts, oatmeal and a small quantity of damaged flour. One general is said to have likened it to peat flavoured with oil. Even this unappetizing ration was denied those who did not bear arms. Paymasters and storemen demanded muskets! Typhus carried off hundreds daily as British men-of-war lobbed shells into the town. The psychologist Masséna forbade military funerals lest they depress the few thousand men remaining to him. After two months news came that Bonaparte was in the plains of Lombardy. Masséna suggested a sortie, but his starving subordinates had not that much fight left in them. Compelled to capitulate, Masséna demanded the honours of war to the astonishment of the Austrian generals. The British admiral, Lord Keith, who greatly admired his defence, insisted that they accept, and on 4 June Masséna rode out on one of the few horses his men had not eaten. His stubborn resistance had paved the way for Bonaparte's great victory at Marengo ten days later.

Masséna was made General-in-Chief of the Armies of Italy and of Reserve (24 June), but he now devoted himself to plundering with such shameless assiduity that his command was given to Brune not two months later (13 August). Masséna was consoled with a pension of 30,000 fr. p.a. (23 September) and a sabre of honour (6 October 1801). From 28 July 1803 to 31 December 1807 he was deputy for the Seine in the Corps Législatif.

When on 19 May 1804 the first list of Marshals of the Empire was published nobody was surprised to see the victor of Zürich included – 'one of eighteen', Masséna drily remarked. And, of course, he was one of the first to receive the Grand Eagle of the Legion of Honour on 2 February 1805.

In the 1805 campaign Masséna commanded the Army of Italy, fighting the indecisive battle of Caldiero (30 October) against the Archduke Charles. Given command of the 8th Corps (11 December) he joined the Grand Army, but almost immediately (28 December) was made commander-in-chief of the Army of Naples, taking up

the command at Bologna on the following 9 January. He invaded
the Kingdom of Naples and took Capua (12 February), entering
Naples with Joseph Bonaparte on the 14th. As commander of the
1st Corps of the Army of Naples he besieged Gaeta from 26 February
until it capitulated on 19 July. In August he directed the expedition
to Calabria, where he was opposed by a partisan, one Michele
Pezza, alias 'Fra Diavolo'.

Meanwhile far away in Berlin on 21 November 1806 Napoleon
signed the decree establishing the Continental Blockade. 'The
British Isles are declared to be in a state of blockade. All commerce
and all correspondence with the British Isles are forbidden.'
Masséna was quick to start a profitable trade in licences, but unfortunately for him the Emperor knew what he was at – and when
the Marshal's hoard was big enough he confiscated it; it is unlikely
that he got the lot. It may be that this episode led to the Marshal's
being called to the Grand Army, which he joined on 12 January
1807. On 24 February he took command of the 5th Corps in place
of Lannes, but on 15 July he obtained leave and went home to Rueil.

On 19 March 1808 Masséna was created Duke of Rivoli. It was
at about this period that Napoleon invited him to take part in a
shoot, an honour the Marshal could well have forgone since his
host succeeded in shooting out one of his piercing black eyes! The
Emperor, whose tactical skill was as yet undiminished, lost no time
in blaming Berthier for the accident.

Commanding the 4th Corps, Masséna played a leading part in
the campaign of 1809. He distinguished himself at Landshut (21
April) and Eckmühl (22 April). On 3 May he took the bridge and
castle of Ebersberg, though at the cost of heavy losses. He covered
himself with glory at the battle of Aspern-Essling, his men defending the great granary of the latter village. When on the evening
of 21 May Lannes accused Bessières of parading about all day
without charging home, Masséna intervened to prevent a duel.
'Put up your swords this instant! You are in my camp and I shall
certainly not permit my soldiers to see the scandalous spectacle of
two marshals drawing on each other in the presence of the enemy!'
It says something for the little man's personality that he could

impose his will on a Gascon blade like Lannes.

At the end of the battle it fell to Masséna to cover the withdrawal of the Grand Army into the Isle of Lobau, an operation which he executed with consummate skill leaving behind not a single one of his wounded.

Soon after this, on 3 July, Masséna on reconnaissance with the Emperor suffered a heavy fall with his horse, which rolled on him, so that he was unable to ride for weeks. He retained his command, however, and at the battle of Wagram was driven about the field in a light carriage, commanding the French left with great success. His carriage, the target of many an Austrian cannoneer, survived intact. But though Masséna cared little for his own safety, that of his young son and A.D.C., Prosper, was a thing very near to his heart. So much so that when a mission of peculiar danger came up the Marshal sent another officer when it was Prosper's turn for duty. To his credit the boy galloped after his fellow A.D.C. When both somewhat surprisingly returned unscathed, a furious Masséna demanded of his son what had made him stick his nose into such a mess, to be told: 'My honour! This is my first campaign. Already I have the cross. What have I done to earn it? Anyway it happened to be my turn.' Doting parent or not, the Marshal had, it seems, brought his son up properly!

Masséna's success at Wagram would have been impossible without his two civilian servants, his coachman and his postilion, whose gallantry demanded some reward. Masséna let it be known that he was going to give them 200 fr. apiece. His staff, well aware of his avarice, pretended to believe that he had annuities in mind. The very suggestion drove the millionaire Marshal almost insane with rage: 'I would sooner see you all shot and get a bullet through my arm! If I listened to you I should be ruined – ruined, you understand?' Unfortunately for him the story reached the ears of the Emperor, whose sense of humour was equal to the occasion. With grave courtesy he complimented Masséna upon his generosity, compelling him to give the two brave men their just reward.

The Marshal also received *his* reward (31 January 1810). He was made Prince of Essling[1] and given the Château de Thouars (Deux-

*Masséna in 1809, with his son Prosper on horseback, and General Fririon, his
chef d'état-major. From the water colour by Carl Agricola.*

Sèvres) – though he declined this last, probably because he did not wish to pay for its repair!

Masséna's last campaign was with the Army of Portugal. To say that he was reluctant to go to Spain would be an understatement. Though only 52, he was beginning to feel a bit antique, and he would have been well content to stay at home and enjoy his riches. Unfortunately for him, he had done so well at Essling and Wagram that Napoleon very reasonably thought him the very man to drive the English leopard into the sea: 'Your reputation alone will suffice to finish the business', he told him.

If Masséna could not enjoy his money in Spain, he could at least indulge his other passion: Madame Leberton, who had been with him in Calabria in 1806, looked charming in her green dragoon uniform.

Masséna left Paris on 29 April and took up his new command at Valladolid on 10 May 1810. On 10 July Ciudad Rodrigo capitulated to him; on 28 August, Almeida. Advancing into Northern Portugal he was bloodily repulsed by Wellington at Busaco (27 September). 'So convinced was Masséna of French invincibility that he had rushed headlong into a battle without proper reconnaissance. He would not make that mistake again.'[1]

Eventually Masséna succeeded in turning Wellington's position, taking Coimbra, which his men pillaged remorselessly (1 October). Pushing on towards Lisbon, he found himself halted by the Lines of Torres Vedras, whose existence he did not so much as suspect until three days before he reached them. The Napoleonic Empire had reached its high-water mark. Masséna reconnoitred the position with the greatest thoroughness, scanning the keypoint of Monte Agraça through a splendid telescope found at Coimbra University, until a British gunner considered he had seen enough and put a shot across his bows. The Marshal politely doffed his hat, mounted, and rode away. He sent for some Portuguese officers of his staff. 'Did you know of this?' They did not and protested that the English must have been busy indeed to construct such formidable fortifications. 'Without doubt, but it was not Wellington that made the mountains.' Masséna hung on near Sobral for a month before withdrawing to a position near Santarém. Eventually he withdrew his starving army towards the Spanish frontier (6 March 1811), with Marshal Ney, the most insubordinate of all his difficult commanders, bringing up the rear. The army was hard-pressed, and poor Madame Leberton ('La poule à Masséna'), bruised by falling off her horse, was dragged along by two soldiers. 'What an idiot I was to bring a woman campaigning!' commented the Marshal. It cannot be said to have been much of an example to his army.

Masséna was nothing if not tenacious. He sent to his fellow marshals for help. But only Bessières came, and he brought with him only 1,500 cavalry, six guns and 30 gun-teams. 'I could do with far more troops and far less Bessières!' said Masséna.

The indecisive battle of Fuentes de Oñoro followed (3 and 5 May 1811). Jac Weller sums up his last campaign:[2]

Masséna and his professional army now had almost a year's experience in fighting Wellington, but had accomplished nothing. ... He had the good sense at both Busaco and Fuentes not to continue unsuccessful attacks indefinitely and expose his army to total defeat. Both Marmont at Salamanca and Napoleon at Waterloo were to make this error.

But if a modern military historian can compare him, to his own advantage, with his great master, Napoleon was impressed by nothing but success. Masséna was recalled and replaced on 7 May by Marmont.

Masséna had fought his last fight. He was given the 8th Military Division at Toulon, an appointment which doubtless left him plenty of time for his main interests. When Napoleon landed in 1815 Masséna sent soldiers hastening after him – very slowly; thus satisfying both Bourbons and Bonapartists that his heart was in the right place. Napoleon made him a peer of France (2 June) and from 22 June to 8 July he commanded the Paris National Guard, and after Waterloo vetoed the idea of a Regency in favour of the King of Rome. He was Governor of Paris (3 July) for a few days, but on the return of the Bourbons he was replaced. He objected to being one of Ney's judges on the grounds that they had quarrelled in 1810.

Wellington and Masséna met in Paris during the Allied occupation.

Masséna:     You turned every hair in my head white.

Wellington:   We were pretty even!

Old beyond his 61 years, the Marshal died in Paris on 4 April 1817.

There is an excellent biography, *Marshal Masséna* (1965) by General Sir James Marshall-Cornwall, K.C.B., C.B.E., D.S.O., M.C.

# PIERRE-FRANÇOIS-CHARLES AUGEREAU, DUC DE CASTIGLIONE
## 1757-1816

Ah! but remember what he did for us at Castiglione!

NAPOLEON

Augereau was low-born and ill-bred, the son of a domestic servant and a fruiterer in the Faubourg Saint-Marceau, Paris, but it is only fair to add that he was a man of spirit, and that a Prussian princess found him courteous and considerate in the dark days after Saalfeld. Above all, when nerves failed at Castiglione, it was Augereau that found the words to inspire Bonaparte and his colleagues to show a brave face.

Augereau was a soldier before the Revolution, but it would be bold to assert that his career can be traced with absolute exactitude. It seems that he joined the *régiment de Clare Irlandais* in 1774 and bought himself out the following year. There is little doubt that in June 1775 he joined the Dragons de Damas (later d'Artois), with whom he served until 1777 when he again bought himself out. He joined the Prussian Army and campaigned against the Austrians and the Turks in the Regiment of Brunswick-Bevern. Returning to the French Army he served in the cavalry regiments of Bourgogne (XX) and the *Carabiniers de Monsieur* (XXII) during 1784–6, quitting them in consequence of certain lapses. In 1786 he went with the Baron de Salis as an instructor to the Neapolitan Army. In 1790 he returned to France and served in the Paris National Guard and then in a Volunteer battalion, before becoming adjutant-major in the *Légion Germanique* (7 September 1792). In 1793 he

AUGEREAU
*From the painting by Robert Lefevre, engraved by T. Johnson.*

came under suspicion and was arrested and detained at Tours, but released on 12 June. Thereafter his advancement was rapid.

26 June: Captain, 11th Hussars.
Waggon-master general of the Army of the Coasts of La Rochelle.

13 September: Lt-Colonel. A.D.C. to General Rossignol in La Vendée.

27 September: Adjutant General. *Chef de brigade*.
Army of the Pyrénées-Orientales.

23 December: General of Division.

During 1794 he saw a certain amount of fighting in the Pyrenees, won an action at Saint-Laurent de la Mouga, when he received several wounds from musket-balls (13 August 1794); besieged Figueras (20 November) and covered the siege of Rosas.

Transferred to the Army of Italy (September 1795), he distinguished himself at Loano (24–5 November), served at Montenotte, Millesimo and Lodi. He particularly distinguished himself at the battle of Castiglione. By 1814 he had convinced himself that he alone was for fighting it out at Lonato and Castiglione whereas Bonaparte and all his other generals wanted to beat a retreat to the south of the River Po. Old soldiers' tales, like wine, improve with age; but one may say in his favour that Napoleon was always prepared to give Augereau full credit for his stand at Castiglione.

After fighting at Arcola, La Favorita and elsewhere Augereau was selected to present the sixty colours captured at Mantua to the Directory.

On 27 July 1797 he left the Army of Italy to take up command of the 17th Military Division at Paris. He had been asked for by the Directory, though his selection was really due to Bonaparte. He and his men played a decisive part in the *coup d'état* of 18 Fructidor year V (4 September 1797). Later, though he opposed Bonaparte's *coup* of 18 Brumaire, he supported the Consulate.

After a series of high commands in Germany and Holland he was unemployed from 23 October 1801 to 29 August 1803, and retired to his estate at La Houssaye (Seine-et-Marne).

On 29 August he was given command of the camp at Bayonne,

and then in January 1804 of the camp at Brest. He was one of the first creation of Marshals of the Empire and received the Grand Eagle of the Legion of Honour.

From 30 August 1805 to 14 February 1807 he commanded the 7th Corps of the Grand Army. He compelled the Austrian general, Jellachich, to capitulate at Feldkirch (November 1805); commanded Napoleon's left at Jena; and won the action of Kolozomb (24 December 1806).

On 6 February 1807 Augereau, who was sick, asked to be relieved of his command, but Napoleon persuaded him to remain at his post for another day – the day of the battle of Eylau, where, besides being shot in the arm, the unhappy Marshal saw his corps practically destroyed before his eyes. He did not spare his comments, and though the Emperor passed this off, as coming from the victor of Castiglione, he did not really forgive him.

Few of those Marshals who were made Dukes were given as their title the name of a victory; Augereau was fortunate, and on 19 March 1808, appropriately enough, Napoleon made him Duke of Castiglione.

Augereau commanded the 7th Corps of the Army of Spain (1 June 1809–24 April 1810), and received the surrender of Gerona on 10 December. He held various commands in Germany, winning a victory at Naumburg (9 October 1813) with the 16th Corps of the Grand Army and serving at Leipzig.

On 5 January 1814 he was made commander-in-chief of the Army of the East (or of the Rhône). Beaten at Saint-Georges on 18 March he was compelled to abandon Lyons five days later. In April he abandoned Napoleon's cause and issued a proclamation in which he insulted him. The restored Bourbons made him a chevalier of Saint-Louis (21 June 1814) and Napoleon on his return from Elba struck his name from the list of Marshals (10 April 1815).

He was a member of the Council of War appointed by the Bourbons to try Marshal Ney, which had the good taste to declare itself 'incompetent'. For this he was disgraced and deprived of his emoluments. He retired to La Houssaye, where he died on 12 June 1816, a fortnight before the reinstatement of Marshal Moncey, who had been dismissed at the same time.

Augereau had a brother, Jean-Pierre Baron Augereau (1772–1836), whose career was not undistinguished.

BERNADOTTE
*From the painting by François Kinson, engraved by T. Johnson.*

# 7

# JEAN-BAPTISTE-JULES BERNADOTTE, PRINCE DE PONTECORVO, LATER KING OF SWEDEN

## 1763–1844

Sergent Belle-Jambe.
*The nickname of Marshal Bernadotte*

Bernadotte was born at Pau on 26 January 1763, the son of a lawyer. He enlisted as a soldier in the Régiment de Brassac on 3 September 1780.

20 May 1782: Grenadier
16 June 1785: Corporal
21 June 1786: *Fourrier* (Quartermaster)
11 May 1788: Sergeant-Major in the Régiment Royal-Marine.

He saved his colonel who was menaced by a Marseille mob, and soon afterwards he was promoted lieutenant in the 36th infantry. He was nevertheless an extreme Republican and had the words 'Mort aux Tyrans' tattooed on his arm!

From 1792 to 1794 he was with the Army of the Rhine, where he became a *chef de bataillon* (13 February 1794). Passing to the Army of the North he served at Fleurus (26 June 1794) and was made a General of Brigade in Kléber's Division (29 June). Very quickly he rose to General of Division and was posted to the Army of the Sambre-et-Meuse (22 October).

In 1795 and 1796 he saw a good deal of fighting on the Rhine without any particular triumph or disaster. Early in 1797 he was sent to Italy, serving at the passage of the Tagliamento and elsewhere, and being sent to present captured Austrian colours to the Directory (3 August).

In February 1798 he was sent as Ambassador to Vienna. On 13 April there was a riot and the French flag was burned: Bernadotte, full of indignation, left the city next day.

On 17 August 1798 Bernadotte married Désirée Clary, sister of Joseph Bonaparte's wife, Julie. Nevertheless he declined to play any part in the coup of 18 Brumaire.

Though made Ambassador to the United States, Bernadotte was prevented from going there by the resumption of hostilities in 1803. He was made Governor of Hanover (14 May 1804) and it was at that time that he raised his handsomely uniformed company of Guides.

Bernadotte was made a Marshal in 1804 and received the Grand Eagle of the Legion of Honour (2 February 1805).

In the 1805 campaign he commanded the 1st Corps of the Grand Army, and in the Manœuvre of Ulm violated Prussian neutrality in the interests of speed. At Austerlitz he commanded the reserve of the centre, and occupied the vital ground which Soult had stormed.

Bernadotte was made Prince of Pontecorvo (5 June 1806), and Grand Dignitary of the *Couronne de Fer* of Italy.

On 14 October 1806 Bernadotte remained inactive between the battlefields of Jena and Auerstädt. Not a man of his corps fired a shot that day. Napoleon was furious, indeed he said at St Helena that he actually signed an order for the Prince's court martial, and according to Marbot, 'The army expected to see Bernadotte severely punished.' But he was married to Desirée Clary whom Bonaparte had loved. 'This business is so hateful', the Emperor wrote to Savary, 'that if I send him before a court martial it will be the equivalent of ordering him to be shot; it is better for me not to speak to him about it; but I shall see that he knows what I think of his conduct. I believe he has enough honour to recognize that he has performed a disgraceful action. . . .' The order for a court martial was torn up. Chandler finds that 'This leniency was proved mistaken by future events.'[1] However that may be, it seems strange that Bernadotte was permitted to retain command of his corps.

So far from being ashamed of his behaviour Bernadotte, like the Gascon he was, told Bourrienne: 'I might have felt piqued at receiving something like orders from Davout, but I did my duty.' This was on 10 November and by that time he had done something to make amends by a remorseless pursuit of the defeated Prussians. He won an action at Halle (17 October), beat Blücher at Nossentin (1 November) and Crivitz (3 November), took Lübeck (6 November) and compelled Blücher to surrender at Schwartau (7 November).

At Lübeck Bernadotte found a Swedish division under Count Mörner, which had landed to support the Prussians. Whilst his soldiers enjoyed themselves plundering the Danish port of Lübeck the Prince of Pontecorvo went out of his way to make a good impression on the Swedes, and permitted them to return home. Marbot writes: 'The Marshal, whose manners, when he liked, were, I must admit, very attractive, was especially desirous to earn the character of a well-bred man in the eyes of these strangers.' Seldom has courtesy been more handsomely repaid.

After winning the combat at Mohrungen (25 January 1807), Bernadotte was wounded in the head by a musket ball on the River Passarge (4 March) and again by a musket ball in the throat at Spanden (5 June). He was compelled to give up command of the 1st Corps.

On 14 July 1807 Bernadotte was made Governor of the Hanseatic Cities. He occupied Jutland and Fünen, and was awarded the Order of the Elephant of Denmark (1808). Part of his force was the Spanish division of the Marquis de la Romaña. Soon after the outbreak of the war in the Peninsula this formation was spirited away by the British Navy, which did not say much for Bernadotte's vigilance.

In 1809 Bernadotte was given command of the Saxon Army (7 March) and this became the 9th Corps of the Grand Army (8 April). The Marshal failed lamentably at Wagram. After being driven back he had the effrontery to boast of what he would have done had he been in supreme command. He then abandoned the key village of

Aderklaa on his own initiative. His Saxons were routed in an attempt to retake it and Bernadotte, galloping in front of them in the hope of rallying them, ran into the Emperor himself. Napoleon may be forgiven for asking, 'Is this the type of "telling manœuvre" by which you will force the Archduke Charles to lay down his arms?' Bernadotte found this unanswerable. 'I hereupon remove you from command of the corps which you have handled so consistently badly,' added the Emperor. 'Quit my presence at once and leave the Grand Army within 24 hours.' It was high time.

Bernadotte reached Paris on 30 July, and on 12 August was chosen by the Council of Ministers to command the army assembled on the River Escaut (Scheldt) to oppose the British expedition to Walcheren. The Emperor disliked a proclamation which the Marshal addressed to his men and summoned him to Vienna. Bernadotte gave up his last French command on 24 September 1809.

On 21 August 1810 the Swedish States-General elected Bernadotte Crown Prince of Sweden, and Napoleon reluctantly agreed to his acceptance. The Swedes were not only grateful for the Marshal's treatment of Mörner's Division in 1806. They hoped that the Emperor might now relax the trade restrictions imposed by his Continental System. The Tsar Alexander, who probably did not know that Napoleon distrusted Bernadotte, saw this development as one more step in a French campaign to surround Russia with enemies.

On 20 October Bernadotte abjured Catholicism. Next day he was presented to the States-General and adopted by King Charles XIII, with the name of Carl Johan (5 November).

In March 1812 Napoleon seized Swedish Pomerania, whereupon in April the Crown Prince of Sweden threw in his lot with the Tsar, promising a benevolent neutrality in exchange for Norway, which then belonged to Denmark.

In 1813 the Crown Prince brought Sweden into the Sixth Coalition against the country of his birth. During the campaign he displayed his usual caution and hesitation, though he did manage to defeat Oudinot at Grossbeeren (23 August) and Ney at Dennewitz (6 September). He fought at Leipzig. He then proceeded to invade

Holstein and compelled the King of Denmark to cede Norway to him by the Treaty of Kiel (14 January 1814).

When Napoleon abdicated for the first time the Crown Prince was not without hopes of taking his place. He was living in a world of his own, for those of his countrymen who knew anything of public affairs regarded him as a traitor – and indeed La Maréchale Lefebvre (Catherine Hubscher, the famous 'Madame Sans Gêne'[2]) told him so to his face. He left Paris for the last time. Having occupied Norway, he played no part in the 1815 coalition against Napoleon.

He was crowned King of Sweden and Norway on 5 February 1818: Charles XIV. On 8 March 1844 he died of apoplexy at Stockholm. He had proved a moderate and efficient ruler, who had the interests of his adopted country very much at heart. He also had the generosity to offer Marshal Ney's eldest son a commission in his army. He founded a popular dynasty which reigns in Sweden to this day. An indifferent French general, he had proved an excellent Swedish king.

# 8

# NICOLAS-JEAN DE DIEU SOULT, DUC DE DALMATIE
## 1769–1851

Le premier manœuvrier d'Europe.

NAPOLEON
*After Austerlitz*
*2 December 1805*

On 26 September 1847 the Duke of Dalmatia, who had been a Marshal for more than forty-three years, and doyen of the marshalate since the death of Moncey in 1842, was promoted to the rank of *Maréchal-Général* – a rank held previously by three men only: Turenne,[1] Villars[2] and Saxe.[3] Whether Soult was quite in their class is, of course, arguable, since his greatest successes were won under the eye of the Emperor, and when he had an independent command he suffered defeat, not once but several times, at the hands of the Duke of Wellington. There are those indeed who would argue that at least four others of Napoleon's Marshals were as good generals as Soult, if not better. But by 1847 Masséna, Davout, Macdonald and Suchet were in their graves. And by that time Soult had become a sort of Grand Old Man of the French Army.

Soult was born at Saint-Amans-La-Bastide (now in Tarn) on 29 March 1769. It is said that his earliest ambition was to be the village baker. At all events, he enlisted as a soldier in the *Régiment Royal-Infanterie* on 16 April 1785.

13 June 1787:　Corporal[4]

31 March 1791: Corporal *fourrier* (Corporal Quartermaster)

1 July 1791:　Sergeant.

During the Revolutionary War Soult rose rapidly, until on 14 May 1794 he was nominated by the Representatives of the People

SOULT
*From the painting by Pierre-Louis de Laval, engraved by T. Johnson.*

to be *adjudant général chef de brigade provisoire* and Chief of Staff of the advanced guard division under Lefebvre. He fought at Fleurus, and was promoted General of Brigade on 11 October 1794.

In the following year Soult was at the siege of Luxembourg (13 April–7 June 1795) and for a while commanded the division of General André Poncet (1755–1838) during his absence.

Soult fought at Altenkirchen and Stockach and was made a provisional General of Division on 4 April 1799 (confirmed 21

77

April). He played a distinguished part in Masséna's great victory of Zürich, and was placed in charge of operations against the great Russian general, Suvorov (3 October).

Soult went to Italy with Masséna and was defeated before Genoa (6 April 1800). In the fighting that followed he was successful more often than not, but ended up with a broken leg, a prisoner of the Austrians (13 May 1800).

In September 1800 Soult was made Governor of Piedmont and checked the insurrection of 'les Barbets', forming from the insurgents themselves a body of gendarmes who pacified the country.

Soult's next command was under Murat in the Army of the South (13 February 1801–1 June 1802). During this period he occupied the Neapolitan ports on the Adriatic and commanded the troops stationed in the Kingdom of Naples.

On 5 March 1802 Soult was made Colonel-General of the Light Infantry of the Consular Guard. From 28 August 1803 to 26 August 1805 he was commandant of the Camp of Saint-Omer.

Soult was promoted Marshal of the Empire on 19 May 1804, and Colonel-General of the Imperial Guard the same day. On 2 February 1805 he was invested with the Grand Eagle of the Legion of Honour.

In the 1805 campaign Soult commanded the 4th Corps and played a decisive stroke at the battle of Austerlitz. 'How long will it take you to move your division to the top of the Pratzen Heights?' the Emperor asked the Marshal at the height of the fighting. 'Less than twenty minutes, Sire, for my troops are hidden at the foot of the valley, hidden by fog and campfire smoke.' 'In that case, we will wait a further quarter of an hour.'

The Emperor, telescope in hand, watched the columns of Kolowrat and Miloradovitch marching south, and when he judged the moment ripe he launched the 4th Corps to the storming of the Pratzen Heights, the vital ground dominating the centre of the battlefield. Soult proved as good as his word, and it was his contribution to this, the most skilful and economical of all the imperial victories, that led Napoleon to call him the ablest tactician in Europe.

Soult commanded the French right at Jena and his corps formed part of the centre at Eylau. 'Marshal,' said the Emperor to him next day, 'the Russians have done us great harm,' to which Soult, nothing daunted, replied, 'And we them. Our cannon balls were not made of cotton.'

Soult served at Heilsberg, and received the capitulation of Königsberg (16 June). At the end of the campaign he was decorated with the Bavarian Order of Saint-Hubert, the Spanish Order of the Golden Fleece and the Swedish Order of the Seraphims, and was awarded pensions amounting to more than 300,000 fr. per annum. Among Napoleon's Marshals, Soult was second only to Masséna in the satisfaction he derived from amassing wealth, and these tributes to his military prowess must have given him great pleasure. He was less pleased with the title bestowed upon him on 29 June 1808. He would much rather have been Duke of Austerlitz than Duke of Dalmatia, but the Emperor regarded some of his victories, notably Marengo and Jena, as falling to his own credit.

From 1808 to 1814 Soult saw a great deal of fighting in the Peninsula. Like most of his fellow Marshals he did not show to much advantage against the British; but it must be remembered that the French tactical system, long successful against the Austrians, the Prussians and the Russians, was inferior to that employed by Moore and Wellington. If an over-simplification may be forgiven, the French column was no match for the British line. It was not altogether the fault of Soult, Masséna and the rest if they employed tactical formations that were standard in the French armies of their day.

Soult's first important engagement with the British was at Corunna, where Lt-General Sir John Moore, K.B. (1761–1809) repulsed him. The French were unable to prevent the embarkation of the British force (16 January 1809). Moore was mortally wounded and Soult had the generosity to raise a monument to his memory.

The Marshal now invaded Portugal and occupied Oporto (29 March). The Duke of Dalmatia was usually a prudent and sensible man, but he was at the same time not lacking in ambition. The previous year had seen Murat made a King, and it occurred to Soult that if so indifferent an officer could rule Naples, he himself could certainly rule Portugal. It is said that he even went so far as to

........................................................................................

## JEAN-BAPTISTE-JULES BERNADOTTE,
Prince de Pontecorvo

........................................................................................

................................................

Aide-de-camp de Bernadotte (left)

................................................

(right) Guide de Bernadotte

organize squads to go about shouting 'Long live King Nicholas!'

Soult's dreams of a throne were rudely shattered when Wellesley suddenly appeared, crossed the River Douro by surprise, and on 12 May compelled the French to evacuate Oporto. The Marshal managed to extricate most of his army, but only because he threw away all its cannon, equipment and baggage in order to escape by mule tracks over the mountains. The Allies suffered no more than 300 casualties, while inflicting upon him a loss of 4,000 men.

Soult now appeared in Castile, winning an action at the bridge of El Arzobispo (8 August). On 16 September he was made Chief of Staff to King Joseph in Jourdan's place, and on 19 November defeated the Spaniards at Ocaña.

In January 1810 the Marshal invaded Andalusia, and in February took Seville, where he set up his Headquarters. He besieged and took Olivença (11–22 January 1811), and then invested Badajoz, which capitulated to him on 11 March. Thereupon, instead of marching to support Masséna in Portugal, he returned to Andalusia. Although his attitude was unco-operative it cannot be asserted that with the addition of Soult's forces the French could successfully have stormed the Lines of Torres Vedras.

Meanwhile Badajoz had been beleaguered by Marshal Sir William Beresford, K.B. (1768–1854) and on 16 May 1811 Soult, attempting to relieve the town, was repulsed by Beresford at Albuera. Outnumbered by the Allies, he won the advantage at the outset but after a fearful contest his men were thrown into confusion and panic by the British infantry.[5] The Allies, British, Portuguese and Spanish, had about 6,000 casualties, and Soult, who admitted no more than 5,936, is thought to have lost about 8,000 [6]

Later in the year the Marshal invaded the kingdom of Grenada, winning the action of Venta del Bahul (9 August). In April 1812 he marched once more to relieve Badajoz, but Wellington had already stormed the place (6 April).

After Wellington's victory at Salamanca (22 July) Soult on 25 August raised the siege of Cadiz which the French had undertaken in 1810, and on 27 August he abandoned Seville, uniting his army with that of Suchet in Valencia on 1 September. Then crossing the

Tagus in October, he took the offensive, re-entered Madrid with King Joseph (2 November) and followed up Wellington's retreating army until it was back under the walls of Ciudad Rodrigo.

The Duke of Dalmatia, though not perhaps a particularly pious man, was nevertheless fond of religious pictures and took back with him from Spain a remarkable collection which he had found time to select despite the arduous nature of his military duties.

Recalled to France on 3 January 1813, Soult was given command of the Old Guard (30 April) and then of the whole Imperial Guard in place of Bessières (2 May). He fought at Bautzen but Napoleon, on hearing the news of Vitoria (fought on 21 June), made him Commander-in-Chief of the Armies in Spain and of the Pyrenees (6 July). He took over his command at Bayonne on 12 July, replacing King Joseph and Marshal Jourdan, and began to reorganize all the French forces in his command. 'Soult was at his very best in such duties; defeated, ill-armed, scattered units were bound into a cohesive whole. Artillery was replaced, ranks filled, and morale restored.'[7] In a stirring address to his men he condemned 'the timid downhearted counsels' of his predecessors, spoke of his men's 'generous enthusiasm, and splendid sense of honour' and ended: 'Soldiers! I sympathize with your disappointment, your grievances, your indignation. I know that the blame for the present situation must be imputed to others. It is your task to repair the disaster.'

That Soult and his men fought well in the months that followed cannot be denied. But the army that had been beaten at Salamanca and Vitoria was up against the victors of those two great fights.

In the battles of the Pyrenees (25 July–1 August) Soult's opening counter-offensive was halted and his army was left even more disorganized than it had been after Vitoria – which is not to say that he was wrong to make the attempt. In the battles of the Nivelle, the Nive and St-Pierre, Wellington compelled Soult, whose logistical difficulties were great, to move his field army inland and quit Bayonne.

At Orthez (27 February 1814) the Allies, numerically inferior, routed Soult's army, which included numbers of ill-trained conscripts, took his guns and baggage and inflicted 4,000 casualties for

*A full-length portrait of Soult showing him in the uniform of colonel-general of the Imperial Guard.*

the loss of 2,164. On 10 April at the battle of Toulouse Wellington took much of Soult's abundant artillery and compelled him to evacuate the city. By that time the war, though they did not know it, was over.

In his defence of south-west France Soult showed himself an able strategist and a good organizer. But the disheartened host he had inherited was no match for the Anglo-Portuguese Army which Wellington had forged in the years since 1808. After Austerlitz Napoleon had called Soult the ablest tactician in Europe. It was in this field especially that he had been out-generalled. Still one can make a case for saying that Soult played a bad hand pretty well. One cannot imagine his predecessors, King Joseph and Jourdan or Marmont, holding out for ten months after the débâcle at Vitoria.

On 19 April 1814 Soult recognized Louis XVIII as King of France and, though he was relieved of his command on 22 April, he was given command of the 13th Military Division at Rennes on 21 June and on 24 September made a commander of Saint-Louis.

From 3 December 1814 to 11 March 1815 Soult was Minister of War. Adhering to Napoleon on his return from Elba, he was made a peer of France (2 June) and Chief of Staff to the Army of the North, an appointment that has been much criticized. No doubt, given a few weeks, so experienced a soldier as Soult would have settled into Berthier's old job with efficiency and authority. But the campaign of 1815 was a *blitzkrieg*. He had no time to play himself in, and since the staff work of Napoleon's Army fell short of the standards of the great days of the Grand Army, the blame must rest to some extent on Soult's shoulders. It is difficult indeed to understand why Napoleon did not give Soult, rather than Ney or Grouchy, command of one of his wings. One can scarcely imagine his bungling Quatre Bras as Ney did.

After Waterloo Soult rallied the remains of the Army at Laon, but, handing over to Grouchy (26 June), he retired to Saint-Amans. His name was struck off the list of Marshals on 27 December and on 12 January 1816 he was exiled and went to Düsseldorf. On 26 May 1819 Soult was authorized to return to France and his rank was restored on 5 January 1820. He was made a peer of France in 1827.

Soult was Minister of War from 1830 to 1834 and President of the Council of Ministers from 1832 to 1834. As Ambassador Extraordinary he attended the Coronation of Queen Victoria in 1838, receiving an enthusiastic welcome from the London crowds. At a reception it is said that the Duke of Wellington stole up behind him, and laying a hand on his arm said: 'Ah, I have you at last!' Soult was Minister of Foreign Affairs and President of the Council from 1839 to 1840.

When in December 1840 the ashes of Napoleon were brought from St Helena to his red granite tomb in Les Invalides, Soult (aged 71), Moncey (aged 86), Oudinot (aged 73), and Grouchy (aged 74), took part in the ceremony, as well as a host of the veterans of the Grand Army.

The old Marshal was once more Minister of War from 1840 to 1845. From 1845 to 1847 he was Minister without Portfolio, and from 1840 to 1847 he was in addition President of the Council.

Eleven days after his retirement, he was given the highest military rank that any Frenchman can earn. He died, aged 82 years and eight months, at his Château of Soultberg in his native commune of Saint-Amans-La-Bastide on 26 November 1851. Soult, the last survivor of the creation of 1804, had his baton for 47 years, six months and seven days, and had lived under seven different political régimes. He, along with Masséna, Davout and Suchet, must certainly be placed in the first rank of the marshals of the Empire. His character was somewhat blemished by ambition and avarice, but he was loyal to the Emperor. Though we hear much of the rivalry between the various marshals, it is pleasant to be able to record that Soult and Mortier were good friends for nearly forty years.

The Marshal-General's younger brother, Pierre-Benoît, Baron Soult (1770–1843), was a cavalry general of some distinction: General of Brigade, 1807; of Division, 1813.

# 9

# GUILLAUME-MARIE-ANNE BRUNE

## 1763–1815

> This General has received seven musket balls in his clothes, none of which wounded him: this is to enjoy good luck!
>
> BONAPARTE
> *After the repulse of an Austrian attack on Verona*
> *1797*

Though a Marshal of the first creation, Brune was far from being *persona grata* with Napoleon, and few of the rewards showered upon his fellows came his way.

Brune was born at Brive-la-Gaillarde (Corrèze) on 13 March 1763. He began life as clerk to the *procureur*, then became a printer and at the outbreak of the Revolution was a journalist in Paris. Well-educated, of an imposing stature and with a decided taste for the career of arms, he soon found himself in a grenadier company. In 1789 he became a captain in the National Guard of Paris.

As a supernumerary adjutant-general *chef de brigade* and Chief of Staff to General Sepher, he won a victory at Pacy-sur-Eure, and soon after became a General of Brigade with the Army of the North (18 August 1793) and fought at Hondschoote. After various commands in France he was sent to Italy (October 1796) and served in Masséna's Division at Arcola and Rivoli. Bonaparte made him a provisional General of Division (17 April 1797), and he was confirmed in that rank by the Directory (7 November 1797).

On 27 January 1798 he was given command of an army on the Swiss frontier, and put down revolts in Berne and Fribourg, though he conducted himself with great moderation, as he did later during his command of the Army of Italy (4 April–31 October 1798).

Summoned to the defence of Holland, where he took command on 9 January 1799, it fell to him to resist the Anglo-Russian expedition of that year. The campaign had its ups and downs: beaten at Alkmaar (2 October) Brune had his revenge at Castricum (6 October), a battle in which he himself led a battalion to the charge. His ardour nearly cost him his life. A Cossack fell upon him lance in hand, but the blow was parried at the last moment by one of Brune's guides, who sabred his assailant, and seizing his horse said to Brune with typical Gallic aplomb: 'Mon général, I present you with a Cossack horse.' The Convention of Alkmaar (18 October) put an end to the operations. The Allies withdrew and 8,000 French and Dutch captives in British prisons were released. The Dutch fleet, however, remained in British hands.

Brune was made a Councillor of State (25 December 1799) and after a brief period in command of the Army of the West (14 January–26 April 1800) he was summoned to Dijon by Bonaparte to command the 18th Military Division and the depots of the Army of Reserve (11 May), during the Marengo campaign. On 13 August he took command of the Army of Italy in place of Masséna. He won an action at Monzembana, at the passage of the Mincio (26 December), took Verona (3 January 1801) and Vicenza and signed the armistice of Treviso. In a campaign of nineteen days his army had slain 10,000 Austrians, and taken 20,000 prisoners, 45 guns, and three colours. Coming just after Moreau's victory at Hohenlinden this was a severe blow to the Austrian monarchy.

Returning to the Council of State, Brune became president of the *section de la guerre*. From 11 September 1802 to 17 December 1804 he was Ambassador to Turkey, and so was abroad when the news of his promotion to Marshal reached him. In 1805 he was invested with the Grand Eagle of the Legion of Honour.

On 15 December 1806 he was made Governor-General of the Hanseatic Cities, and on 29 April 1807 of the *corps d'observation* of the Grand Army. On 15 July he took Stralsund. He was disgraced for having, in a convention with the Swedish Army, spoken of the French Army instead of the Army of 'Sa Majesté Impériale et Royale'. He remained unemployed until 1814, when, under-

BRUNE
*From the portrait by Bataille, after Mme Benoist, engraved by E. Heinemann.*

standably, he adhered to the Bourbons and was made chevalier of Saint-Louis (1 June 1814).

After Napoleon's return from Elba Brune was made Governor of Provence and commander of the 8th Military Division in Masséna's place (11 April 1815); then commander of the Corps of Observation on the Var (17 April). Napoleon made him a peer of France on 2 June, and he kept the tricolour flying over Toulon until the end of July, when his arrest was ordered. On his way to Paris he was attacked at Avignon by a mob of Royalist extremists (*la bande de Trestaillons*). He was killed by a carbine shot, stabbed a hundred times by these wretches' poignards and thrown into the Rhône, where for more than an hour his corpse was the mark for their musketry.

According to Las Casas, Napoleon described Brune as 'Un déprèdateur intrépide' – a bold plunderer. But this seems to be an undeserved slur upon the honour of a brave and efficient officer whose ideas did not always coincide with those of the Corsican.

# JEAN LANNES, DUC DE MONTEBELLO

## 1769–1809

> In Marshal Lannes we lost one of the most gallant men our armies could boast of. His life was too short for his friends, but his career of honour and glory was without parallel.
>
> GENERAL SAVARY[1]

Lannes was born at Lectoure (Gers) on 10 April 1769, and apprenticed to a dyer. In 1792 he enrolled as a volunteer in the 2nd battalion of Gers, in which he became *sous-lieutenant* of grenadiers (20 June). He served in the Army of the *Pyrénées Orientales* from 1793 to 1795. In 1793 he was promoted three times: lieutenant (25 September); captain of grenadiers (31 October); *chef de brigade* (25 December). In a fight at Banyuls a musket ball went right through one of his arms. In 1794 he fought at the taking of Montesquiou (30 April) and at Saint-Laurent de la Mouga (13 April).

Transferred to the Army of Italy Lannes fought at Loano, Millesimo and Dego, and was given command of four battalions of grenadiers forming the advanced guard under General Dallemagne (5 May). He was the first man across the Po at Plasencia, and fought at Lodi. He beat the insurgents of Pavia at Binasco and burnt the village (26 May). He served under Dallemagne in the attack on San-Giorgio (4 June), and Bonaparte made him provisional General of Brigade in the cavalry (September).

Lannes took two colours at Bassano, and was wounded by a musket shot at Governolo (15 September) and by three shots at Arcola. In 1797 he had successes on the Senio (3 February) and before Ancona (9 February) and was confirmed in the rank of General

91

of Brigade by the Executive Directory (17 March).

Though intended for the Army of England, he went with Bonaparte to the Army of the Orient, serving in the attack on Malta (10 June 1798). Lannes was at the capture of Alexandria, occupied Rosetta, and played a part in putting down the revolt in Cairo (21 October). In 1799 he commanded a division in the Syrian campaign. He distinguished himself at the capture of El 'Arish (20 February), at the storming of Jaffa (7 March) and was shot in the neck in an assault on Acre (8 May). Two days later Bonaparte made him a provisional General of Division.

Lannes recovered in time to serve at Abukir (25 July) and was shot in the leg at the siege of the Fort of Abukir (27 July). On 22 August he embarked with Bonaparte for France.

Lannes supported the *coup* of 18 Brumaire when he commanded the Headquarters at the Tuileries (9 November). From 12 November to 27 December 1799 he was *commandant extraordinaire* of the 9th and 10th Military Divisions. Thus in a time of crisis Bonaparte ensured that key positions were in safe hands.

Lannes's loyalty earned him the appointment of Inspector General of the Consular Guard (16 April 1800). A decree of the consuls of 10 May confirmed him in the rank of General of Division, and Bonaparte gave him command of the advanced guard of the Army of Reserve during the Marengo campaign. He showed great activity and achieved a number of successes after the passage of the Great Saint-Bernard Pass, most notably his victory at the battle of Montebello (9 June). At Marengo he held the Austrian attack for seven hours and Bonaparte awarded him a sabre of honour.

On 14 November 1802 Lannes was named minister plenipotentiary and envoy extraordinary to Portugal, but his mission failed to establish the rights of French merchant vessels in the Tagus, and he returned to France, and was given command of the Camp at Ambleteuse (4 July 1803).

Lannes was one of the first creation of Marshals. He received the Grand Cross of Portugal (1805), the Grand Eagle of the Legion of Honour (2 February), and was made commander of the *Couronne de Fer* (25 February 1806).

LANNES
*From the painting by Jean-Baptiste-Paulin Guérin, engraved by G. Kruell.*

As commander of a Corps of the Grand Army Lannes served in the campaigns of 1805–7. He took part in the capture of Ulm and commanded the French left at Austerlitz. He defeated Prince Louis Ferdinand of Prussia at Saalfeld (10 October), commanded Napoleon's centre at Jena, and was slightly wounded at Pultusk (26 December 1806). He now fell ill and gave up command of the 5th Corps (January 1807). His services were rewarded with the Grand Cross of the Order of Saint Henry of Saxony. On his recovery he was given the Reserve Corps (5 May 1807) with which he assisted at the siege of Danzig (26 May). He was at the battle of Heilsberg and commanded the centre at Friedland.

Lannes was well rewarded for his services.

30 June 1807: Pension of 177,820 fr. a year from the Grand Duchy of Warsaw.

13 September 1807: Colonel-General of the Swiss regiments. Chevalier of the Order of Saint-Andrew of Russia.

10 March 1808: Pensions of 100,000 fr. from Westphalia and 50,000 fr. from Hanover.

15 June 1808: Duke of Montebello.

Lannes was now, like many of his colleagues, a rich man. It would not be strange had he wished to live for a while in peace and enjoy his hard-won wealth and honours. Instead he soon found himself campaigning in Spain (October 1808). He defeated Castaños at Tudela (23 November), but soon afterwards his horse fell with him down a precipitous slope and he had to give up his command (2 December). Larrey, the famous surgeon, had him sewn up in a fresh sheepskin and this remarkable treatment worked. On 20 December he took command of the Siege of Saragossa which surrendered to him on 21 February.

Summoned to the Grand Army, he served at Abensberg (20 April 1809), at the capture of Landshut (21 April), at Eckmühl, and at the storming of Ratisbon, where he greatly distinguished himself.

At the battle of Essling his corps (2nd) held out well all day. In the evening whilst he was sitting resting a cannon-ball struck him on the knees. He underwent amputation, but succumbed to his wounds at Ebersdorff, near Vienna, on 31 May. It is said that when Napoleon visited him on his death-bed he urged him to make peace. Lannes was on very familiar terms with the Emperor, who permitted him – and him alone – to address him with 'tu', instead of 'vous'. A Prussian princess who met him just after Saalfeld found him rude and inconsiderate, and it may be that his manners were those of a grenadier rather than a duke. Napoleon felt his loss keenly, and it is not likely that had he lived, he would have thrown in his lot with Marmont in 1814.

Lannes's body was taken back to France and Jean-Roch Coignet,

*Napoleon visits the wounded Lannes after the battle of Essling. From the painting by E. Boutigny, engraved by W. B. Closson.*

then an N.C.O. in the Grenadiers of the Guard, describes his obsequies:

'After a fortnight's rest in the fine barracks of Courbevoie, all in new clothes, we were reviewed by the Emperor at the Tuileries. Preparations were being made for the burial of Marshal Lannes. A hundred thousand men formed the funeral cortège of this celebrated warrior, which started from the Gros Caillou to go to the Panthéon. I was one of the non-commissioned officers who bore the bier. Sixteen of us carried it down eight or ten steps on the left side of the wing of the Panthéon, and there placed it on some trestles. The whole army marched in front of the remains of this brave soldier. The procession was passing till midnight.'

# JEAN LANNES,
Duc de Montebello

..............................................................................

# LOUIS-GABRIEL SUCHET,
## Duc d'Albufera

..............................................................................

# ÉDOUARD-ADOLPHE-CASMIR-JOSEPH MORTIER, DUC DE TRÉVISE

## 1768–1835

The big mortar has a short range.

*Grand Army joke*

Mortier's range was up to the command of a corps, and that he did very well. He was a big, stolid, friendly sort of man, the son of a cloth merchant who had married an Englishwoman.

Born at Le Cateau-Cambrésis (Nord) on 13 February 1768, Mortier, who was destined for commerce, studied at the *Collège des Anglais* at Douai and proved a good scholar. He spoke English as well as French.

At the outbreak of the Revolution he joined the National Guard of Dunkerque (1789–91). His father, Antoine-Charles-Joseph Mortier, was deputy of the Third Estate for Cambrésis in the States-General.

On 1 September 1791 Mortier was elected captain in the 1st Battalion of *Voluntaires du Nord*. His first campaigns were with the Army of the North (1792–4). He was with Dumouriez at Jemappes and at the capture of the citadel of Namur (21 November 1792). In the following year he fought at Neerwinden and at Hondschoote (8 September). On 15 October he was wounded by grapeshot at Dourlers.

In 1794 he served at Fleurus (26 June), and was then transferred to the Army of the Sambre-et-Meuse (1794–7). At the siege of Maestricht in November he compelled Fort Saint-Pierre to surrender. Promoted *adjudant-général chef de brigade* (13 June 1795),

**MORTIER**
*From the painting by Marie-Nicolas Ponce-Camus, engraved by E. Heinemann.*

he distinguished himself under Marceau at the passage of the Rhine at Neuwied (15 September). Next year in command of Lefebvre's outposts he drove the Austrians back in confusion across the River Archer (31 May 1796). He served at Altenkirchen, where Marceau fell (4 June). On 4 July he captured 600 Austrians at Willendorf, and negotiated the capitulation of Frankfurt-am-Main (13 July). In the combat at Hirscheid (8 August) he commanded the cavalry in place of General Antoine Richepanse (1770–1802), who had been wounded two days previously. He seems to have been a success in his rôle for on 16 January 1797 he was made *chef de brigade* of the 23rd Regiment of Cavalry.

In April 1797 Mortier was serving under Lefebvre, and negotiated the occupation of Mainz by the French. After the Peace of Campo Formio, with a modesty unusual among the twenty-six future Marshals, he declined the rank of General of Brigade.

In 1798 Mortier was Lefebvre's Chief of Staff with the Army of Mainz, and was eventually promoted General of Brigade on 23 February 1799. He fought in Lefebvre's Division at Stockach (25 March). In June he was in Soult's Division and on 28 August was given command of the 4th Division of the *Armée du Danube et d'Helvétie*, with which he served at Zurich (25–6 September), and Masséna made him a provisional General of Division (25 September). After being repulsed at Schwyz he won an action at Rosemberg in the Muotathal (1 October). He was given command of the 3rd Division under Soult (3 October) and confirmed in his rank by the Executive Directory (19 October). Then after a brief spell with the Army of the Rhine he was posted to the 17th Military Division in Paris (15 April 1800).

As Lieutenant-General of the First Consul he was put in charge of the occupation of Hanover (3 May 1803), a task which he brought to a successful conclusion when the Hanoverian Army capitulated at Artlenbourg (4 July). It was probably at this time that he was permitted to raise the troop of Guides, whose handsome uniform, perhaps designed by Mortier himself, is illustrated.

On 2 February 1804 Mortier was made Colonel-General of the Artillery and the Sailors of the Consular (and later the Imperial)

Guard. He was one of the eighteen Marshals of the Empire promoted on 19 May 1804 and was made commandant of the 2nd Cohort of the Legion of Honour (14 June) and invested with the Grand Eagle (2 February 1805), as well as being made a chevalier of the Order of Christ of Portugal. On 30 August 1805 he was given command of the infantry of the Imperial Guard.

From 7 November to 16 December 1805 the Marshal was in command of a provisional corps of the Grand Army at whose head he fought against tremendous odds at Dürrenstein (11 November) and covered himself with glory. It was a desperate affair and, when the fighting was at its height, Mortier was seen at the head of a valiant band of grenadiers, laying about him with his sword like any trooper.

In command of the 8th Corps of the Grand Army (1 October 1806–12 July 1807) Mortier conquered Hesse and Hanover, occupied Bremen and Hamburg (19 October), won an action at Anklam (16 April 1807) and laid siege to Colberg. He commanded the left wing at Friedland.

On 2 July 1808 Mortier was created Duke of Treviso and awarded 100,000 francs a year (to be paid by Hanover).

The Marshal was given command of the 5th Corps of the Army of Spain (2 October) and was the real victor of Somosierra (30 November). He then covered Lannes's siege of Saragossa (January–March). He did well that year – which is more than can be said of most of his fellow Marshals – for he helped Soult win the action at the bridge of Arzobispo (8 August) and was wounded at the battle of Ocaña when King Joseph and Soult with 30,000 men defeated 53,000 Spaniards under General Areizaga.

Mortier took part in Soult's conquest of Andalusia, and summoned Badajoz (9 February 1810), but in vain. Victor in the combat at Fuente de Cantos (15 September), he covered the siege of Badajoz, which capitulated on 11 March 1811. He won the battle of Gebora (19 February 1811), and successfully besieged Campo Maior (21 March).

Recalled to France in May 1811, Mortier commanded the Young Guard in Russia, and served at Borodino. He was Governor of

Moscow, and worked energetically to fight the fires and to check pillage. When he evacuated Moscow Napoleon gave Mortier the task of blowing up the Kremlin – which is still there – and commanding the rearguard. He served throughout the retreat and assumed command of the Imperial Guard under Prince Eugène on 22 January 1813. During the 1813 campaign he commanded the Young Guard at Lützen, Bautzen, Wurschen, Dresden, Leipzig and elsewhere.

In the Campaign of France the Marshal commanded the Old Guard (December 1813–April 1814) taking a creditable part in all the fighting and notably in Marmont's defence of Paris. He was not one of those Marshals that brought pressure upon the Emperor to abdicate and he was one of the few to visit him and pay his respects before he departed for Elba.

The Bourbons made Mortier a chevalier of Saint-Louis (1 June 1814), a peer of France (4 June) and Governor of the 14th Military Division at Lille (21 June).

When Napoleon returned from Elba, Mortier met King Louis XVIII at Lille and escorted him to the frontier. Napoleon then gave him command of the Old Guard but he fell ill with sciatica at Beaumont and took no part in the campaign – except that he sold two of his chargers to Marshal Ney. His place was taken very adequately by General Antoine, Comte Drouot (1774–1847).

Mortier's name was expunged from the list of peers of France (24 July 1815), but soon after he was made a member of the court martial convened to try Marshal Ney. At first he said he would sooner be cashiered, but then agreed to serve. The Court declared itself invalid, with the best intentions, but Ney's fate would have been safer in its hands than in those of his peers. Mortier was dismissed from command of the 16th Military Division (27 December). But he was not long in this ill-merited disgrace. On 10 January 1816 he was given the 15th Military Division at Rouen.

In 1819 he was made a peer of France once more and in 1820 a commander of Saint-Louis. In 1825 he was made a chevalier of the *ordres du roi* (Saint-Esprit, Saint-Michel etc.), and in 1828 a member of the *conseil supérieur de la guerre*.

At the coronation of King Louis-Philippe it was Mortier that presented the sword, the traditional function of the Constable of France.

In 1830 and 1832 the Marshal was Ambassador to Russia, and in 1831 he was made Grand Chancellor of the Legion of Honour. In 1834 for a brief period he was Minister of War.

On 28 July 1835 the Marshal was in the royal cortège reviewing the National Guard in the boulevard du Temple when he was killed by Fieschi's infernal machine. He was the last of the twenty-six Marshals created by the Emperor Napoleon I to die a violent death. Far away in Stockholm the King of Sweden mourned the death of an old comrade. So in France did Soult, who had learned to value him before ever Napoleon Bonaparte became an Emperor. Of all the Marshals it may be asserted that the Duke of Treviso had the fewest enemies.

# MICHEL NEY, DUC D'ELCHINGEN, PRINCE DE LA MOSKOVA
## 1769–1815

Le Brave des Braves.

**NAPOLEON**
*21 November 1812*

Ney's part in the retreat from Moscow and at Waterloo have made him the most famous of all Napoleon's Marshals. It would be a mistake, however, to think that 'the bravest of the brave' was simply a hot-headed *sabreur*. He was in addition a skilful corps commander with a genuine interest in his profession and a considerable knowledge of the Art of War. At the same time he was undeniably a romantic. And as for politicians he neither understood nor liked them.

Michel Ney was born at Sarrelouis (Moselle) on 10 January 1769, and unattracted by the trade for which his parents intended him – that of a barrel-cooper – enlisted, voluntarily, in the *Régiment Colonel-Général des Hussards*[1] (12 February 1787).

1 January 1791:    *Brigadier fourrier* (Corporal Quartermaster).

1 February 1792:    *Maréchal des logis chef.*[2]

14 June 1792:    *Adjudant sous-officier* (R.S.M.).

From 1792 to 1794 he was with the Army of the North, being appointed provisional A.D.C. to General François-Joseph Drouot, *dit* Lamarche (1733–1844) (14 October 1792).

29 October 1792:    *Sous-lieutenant*, 5th Hussars.

5 November 1792:    Lieutenant, 5th Hussars.

3 February 1793:    A.D.C.

NEY
*From a copy of the painting by François Gérard, engraved by R. G. Tietze.*

18 March 1793:    Served at Neerwinden.

1 August 1793:    Rejoined the 5th Hussars, as his general had been suspended.

12 April 1794:    Elected captain.

Ney was given command of a party of 500 horse under Kléber in May. Posted to the Army of the Sambre-et-Meuse (28 June 1794), he was nominated *adjudant général chef d'escadrons* (31 July), his rank being confirmed by the Committee of Public Safety (9 September). Promoted *adjudant général chef de brigade* (15 October), he served at the siege of Maastricht, where he was shot in the left shoulder (22 December).

On 8 September 1795 Ney defeated the *émigrés* at Opladen. The following year he was in the combat at Altenkirchen (4 June). On 15 July he took Würzburg and its citadel. He distinguished himself in the combat at Forchheim, and on 1 August was promoted General of Brigade. In 1797 he commanded the body of hussars belonging to the Army of the Sambre-et-Meuse under General Paul Grenier (1768–1827), who like Ney was born at Saarelouis.

He was in a number of actions in April, winning one at Kirchberg (19 April), but was taken prisoner at Giessen on the 21st. Exchanged on 27 May, he does not appear to have been in action again until the capture of Mannheim early in 1799. Promoted General of Division (28 March), he was first given command of the light cavalry of the *Armées d'Helvétie et du Danube* (4 May), then of the advanced guard division under Oudinot (23 May); but being wounded in the thigh and the hand at Winterthur (27 May), he was obliged to give up his command next day.

From 25 September to 24 October 1799 Ney was provisionally in command of the Army of the Rhine, with which he continued to serve for over a year, seeing a lot of fighting. He was wounded twice at Mannheim (1799) and played a decisive part in General Jean-Victor Moreau's great victory at Hohenlinden.

Ney commanded the French army in Switzerland (28 September 1802), was made Minister Plenipotentiary, occupied Zürich and signed the Act of Mediation with the Swiss Republic (19 February 1803).

In 1803 Napoleon gave Ney command, first of the Camp of Compiègne (29 August), then of the Camp of Montreuil (28 December). He was one of the Emperor's first promotion of 18 Marshals, and was given the Grand Eagle of the Legion of Honour (2 February 1805).

In the Austrian campaign of 1805 the Marshal commanded the 6th Corps, with which he greatly distinguished himself at Elchingen

(14 October). He had on his staff the celebrated Swiss military historian and theorist, Antoine-Henri Jomini (1779–1869), then a *chef de bataillon.*[3] Jomini, who had made a careful study of the wars of Frederick the Great and of Napoleon's campaign of 1796, understood the Emperor's strategy as well as any man, and far better than most of the Marshals. He had shown the manuscript of his *Traité des grandes opérations militaires*[4] to Murat, and others, only to be rebuffed. But he found Ney much more open-minded and generous. Ney read his work with great interest, advanced him money to pay for its publication, and permitted him to accompany him as a volunteer A.D.C., until a commission could be obtained for him. Ney put Jomini in charge of his private office, with the special task of preparing the daily orders of march.

Napoleon opened the 1805 campaign with a great manœuvre to cut off the Austrian, General Mack von Leiberich, who had some 30,000 men at Ulm, from Vienna and the Tirol. Ney, whose 6th Corps was supposed to block the escape route along the north bank of the Danube, was ordered to the south by Murat. Jomini had, however, given Ney an insight into the Emperor's strategy and the Marshal protested. There was an angry scene and Murat added one more to his already considerable band of lifelong enemies. In fact when Mack did make an attempt to break out Ney foiled him in brilliant fashion at Elchingen (14 October), the combat from which his ducal title was to be taken (6 June 1808).

To Ney fell the task of invading the Tirol. Driving back the Archduke Johann, he took Innsbruck on 7 November.

In the Prussian campaign of 1806 Ney distinguished himself at Jena by attacking before he was meant to and nearly getting himself cut off. 'The Emperor was very much displeased at Marshal Ney's obstinacy. He said a few words to him on the subject – but with delicacy' (General Savary). In the pursuit after the battle the Marshal took Erfurt (15 October) with 14,000 men and 100 guns; and compelled Magdeburg to capitulate with its garrison of 22,000 men with 600 guns (8 November).

On 2 January 1807, despite strict orders forbidding any forward movement until the spring, Ney advanced from his bivouac area

*A drawing by Meissonier of Ney surrounded by his staff.*

around Neidenburg and swept the Polish lakeland round Allenstein as far as Heilsberg, in search of supplies. This may have decided the Russian General Bennigsen to make a winter offensive. At any rate Napoleon blamed Ney, though in fact the Russians, being better able to cope with winter conditions than Frenchmen or Germans, often profit by that advantage.

There followed the bloody battle of Eylau, the first decided check to the Grand Army. The head of Ney's column did not reach the field until 7 p.m. but its onslaught put new heart into the French, and decided Bennigsen to quit the field.

At Guttstadt on 1 March with 14,000 men the Marshal held at bay a force of Russians estimated at 70,000.

At Friedland Ney commanded the French right, playing a decisive part, and in the words of Napoleon's bulletin 'setting an example to the corps which is always distinguished, even among the fine Army Corps of the Grand Army'. Berthier, in a letter home, wrote: 'You can form no idea of Ney's brilliant courage – equalled only in the age of chivalry. It is to him chiefly that we owe the success of this memorable day.'

Between 30 June 1807 and 10 March 1808 Ney was awarded pensions amounting to nearly 300,000 francs a year.

The Duke of Elchingen was called to the Army of Spain (2 August 1808) and given command of the 6th Corps, with which he took Bilbao (26 September). The Emperor blamed him, unjustly, for the escape of Castaños in November. On 28 December Ney's Corps was leading the pursuit of Sir John Moore's Army. The Emperor himself, too near the forefront for safety, was the first man into Valderas, escorted by a single squadron of the Chasseurs of the Guard. Ney, ever frank, was not afraid to rebuke him: 'Sire, I thank Your Majesty for acting as my advanced guard.' In May 1809 he chased the Marquis de la Romaña from the Asturias; and won the action at Baños (12 August). Ney commanded the 6th Corps in Masséna's Army of Portugal (17 April 1810) and proved a difficult subordinate. He besieged and took Ciudad Rodrigo (6 June–10 July), and Almeida (24 July–28 August) and drove the Light Division back across the River Coa (24 July). When he tried to follow up his success by pressing three determined attacks across a narrow bridge he lost 400 men to no purpose. It was his first encounter with British troops. At Busaco he attacked on both sides of the Great Ravine. His northern columns were repulsed by the Light Division and disintegrated into a panic-stricken rabble.[5] His southern attack, though not broken, was halted 100 yards from the Portuguese position and never came to grips.

Ney detested Masséna and his conduct during the campaign was nothing short of insubordinate, but when the French retreated from Portugal, Ney commanded the rearguard and did so with great skill. When they neared the frontier Masséna, in order to save face, wanted to remain in Portugal and moved south-east to Guarda, instead of east to Almeida. Ney disapproved so violently that Masséna relieved him of his command for insubordination (23 March), and he was sent home to France. Beyond question he deserved it. 'Le rougeaud' (the redheaded one), as the soldiers called him, could upon occasion be hot-tempered beyond reason.

From 31 August 1811 to 1 February 1812 Ney was in command of the Camp of Boulogne. He was then given command of the 3rd Corps of the Grand Army (1 April), which he led at Krasnoe (4 August) where the King of Naples blocked the progress of the corps by a series of futile cavalry charges. The Russians were able to withdraw in good order. His men were the first into Smolensk at the end of the battle for that city (17 August). At Borodino Ney's[6] corps was in the heaviest of the fighting against Bagration, and when the latter fell the French made some progress for a number of the Russian troops lost heart and abandoned their positions. In vain Davout and Ney asked Napoleon to launch the Imperial Guard and exploit their success: the Emperor who had a heavy cold was listless and uncertain. Borodino led to the capture of Moscow, but it failed to destroy the main Russian field army.

On 19 October Napoleon left Moscow and the great retreat, in which Ney was to show all his best qualities, began. It was not until 3 November that the Emperor ordered him to take over command of the rearguard from Davout, but from then on his was the post of danger. That day came the first flurries of snow. On 8 November

Prince Eugène wrote of his own corps: 'Three days of suffering have so dispirited the men that at this moment I believe them incapable of any serious effort. Numbers have died of hunger or cold, and many more in their despair have permitted themselves to be taken by the enemy.' The rearguard was hampered by a horde of some 30,000 stragglers. By the time it reached Smolensk the Grand Army which had left Moscow nearly 100,000 strong was down to about 41,500. Of Ney's 10,000 men only 3,000 were still in the ranks. But the Emperor reinforced him and when on 17 November he marched from Smolensk he had 6,000 men, 12 guns and a squadron of cavalry under his command.

It was now that Ney's difficulties began. The Emperor, hastening to secure the crossings of the River Berezina, lost touch with his rearguard. When the Marshal, albeit with only 900 men, unexpectedly turned up at Orsha on the evening of 21 November Napoleon's morale soared at the well-nigh incredible news. 'I have, then, saved my eagles!' he cried – though the logic of the remark is not obvious – going on to say that he would have given the 300 million francs in his treasury rather than lose such a man. It was then that he bestowed upon Ney the title of 'the bravest of the brave'. He had merited it. When on 18 November General Miloradovitch, who had cut him off, sent an officer to demand his surrender Ney was brief with him. 'A Marshal of France never surrenders. One does not parley under the fire of the enemy. You are my prisoner.' Unable to break through, the Marshal had numerous bivouac fires made and slipped away under cover of darkness. When the hetman Platov set upon him with a swarm of Cossacks, Ney formed his men in square, and marched on through the snow – a most difficult manœuvre even on a parade ground. Unquestionably Ney's gallantry raised the morale of all those who were still trying to put up a fight.

Reinforced to a strength of 3,000, Ney fought at the passage of the Berezina (28 November), taking command of Oudinot's men in addition to his own when the latter was wounded.

As the weather worsened straggling increased until there were only some 13,000 men in the ranks (2 December) and Ney's rear-

MICHEL NEY,
Duc d'Elchingen, Prince de la Moskova

...................................................................

**ÉDOUARD-ADOLPHE-CASIMIR-JOSEPH MORTIER,**
Duc de Trévise (left)

...................................................................

(right) Guide de Mortier

*'Marshal Ney sustaining the rearguard of the Grand Army', from the painting by
Adolphe Yvon, engraved by Henry Wolf.*

guard had shrunk to 100 men. He and General Maurice-Étienne, Baron Gérard, ensconced behind a palisade, held Kowno Bridge for several hours (13 December). Coignet, who saw it, writes: 'A retreat was urgently necessary; Marshal Ney effected it at nine o'clock at night, after having destroyed all that remained of our artillery, ammunition, and provisions, and having set fire to the bridges. It may be said in praise of Marshal Ney that he kept the enemy at bay at Kowno by his own bravery. I saw him take a musket and five men and face the enemy. The country ought to be grateful for such men.' The last Frenchman to quit Russian soil was the Duke of Elchingen.

Ney soon had a new title: Prince of the Moskwa[7] (25 March 1813), and a stupendous pension of 800,000 francs to be paid by Rome, the Mont de Milan, Westphalia and Hanover (8 February). No doubt after his exertions in Russia he would like to have enjoyed his wealth and honours in peace. But it was not to be. By the end of April he was back in action again, at Weissenfels (29 April). Though wounded by a shot in the right leg at Lützen, he still found no rest – unless the twenty-four hours given him to reorganize his shattered formations can be so described.

Ney commanded Napoleon's left at Bautzen, but his costly attack on the strong defences of the village of Preititz – made against the advice of his Chief of Staff, Baron Jomini – was a stupid blunder. Bautzen was a victory for Napoleon and his new and inexperienced army, but the mistakes of subordinates, including Ney, robbed him of its fruits.

At Dresden the Marshal was in temporary command of two divisions of the Old Guard, and fought with marked success in the French centre.

A few days later (2 September) the Emperor ordered Ney to march on Berlin, but was unable to give him the 80,000 troops Ney thought necessary for the task. On 6 September Ney blundered into a trap set for him by Bernadotte at Dennewitz, and, with the instincts of an old hussar, tried to solve his problems by plunging sword in hand into the fight. He lost 10,000 men to his enemy's 7,000.

Ney commanded the northern sector in the battle of Leipzig, being wounded on 18 October and authorized to return to France on the 23rd. He recovered in time to take part in much of the fighting during the campaign of France, Brienne, La Rothière, Champaubert, Montmirail, Château-Thierry, Craonne, Laon, Reims, Châlons-sur-Marne, Arcis-sur-Aube. . . . He was the spokesman of the group of Marshals who, after the fall of Paris, pressed Napoleon to abdicate and was one of those authorized to negotiate with the Tsar.

After the first abdication he adhered to the Bourbons and was made Governor of the 6th Military Division at Besançon (21 May), chevalier of Saint-Louis (1 June) and a peer of France (4 June 1814).

When Napoleon returned from Elba Ney was ordered to arrest him, and declared, in his rash, unthinking way, that he would put him in an iron cage. Then, finding that everywhere the rank and file were welcoming the Emperor, he remembered the rebuffs that his wife had met with at court, and changed sides himself (12 March). At first Napoleon did not employ him except to inspect the frontier between Lille and Landau, though he made him a peer (2 June). At the last moment, however, the Emperor summoned Ney to the Army of the North (11 June) and he hurried to the front so ill-prepared that he was compelled to buy two chargers from Mortier, who had fallen sick.

Given command of the left wing at Quatre Bras, Ney hesitated for the first time in his life and bungled badly, thinking no doubt that the British were concealing their strength as at Busaco, when in fact they simply had not arrived.

At Waterloo he was under the eye of the Emperor, and if he threw away the flower of the French cavalry in charge after charge against Wellington's squares, it is difficult to see why Napoleon, who was but a few hundred yards away, could not have stopped him had he thought of a better plan. Ney had four horses shot under him, left the field hatless, exhausted and on foot, and owed his escape to the generosity of a major of the Red Lancers, who gave him his last spare horse.

*The execution of Ney in the Luxembourg Gardens, 8 December 1815. From the painting by M. Goubaud.*

Ney could easily have escaped abroad, and King Louis XVIII would have been saved much embarrassment had he done so. Instead he took refuge at the Château de la Bessonie (Cantal) where he was arrested (3 August). He was brought before a Council of War whose members included Jourdan, Masséna, Augereau and Mortier. But Ney was a peer of France and insisted on his right to be tried by his peers. In fact he would have been much wiser to confide his fate to his former comrades in arms, for, as Davout said, no soldier of them would condemn such a man – 'Not even Ragusa'. However, after much legal quibbling the court, greatly to the relief of its members, was declared incompetent. 'We were cowards', said Augereau. 'We ought to have insisted upon our right in order to save him from himself.'

Ney's trial took place on 4 December and on 6 December the Peers found him guilty by 107 votes to 47. Of the Peers 109, including Kellermann, Pérignon, Sérurier, Victor and Marmont, voted for the death penalty. The last two names will surprise nobody, but one might have hoped that the other three would have behaved better.

On the morning of 7 December 1815 the Prince of the Moskwa was shot at the Carrefour de l'Observatoire in the Jardins du Luxembourg. He himself gave the order to fire, and was struck by eleven bullets. One of the soldiers had the good taste to hit the top of the wall.

# LOUIS NICOLAS DAVOUT, DUC DE D'AUERSTÄDT ET PRINCE D'ECKMÜHL
## 1770–1823

This Marshal displayed distinguished bravery and firmness of character, the first qualities in a warrior.

NAPOLEON
*Fifth Bulletin of the Grand Army*
*15 October 1806*

Marshal Davout's visit has been got over; it was a weary business trying to enliven him, for it is impossible to be more stolid and uncommunicative than was this thoroughly unpleasant man. His face betrays that he can be very harsh and brutal though not specially spiteful or intellectual. His A.D.C.s were as unamiable as the Marshal himself.

DUCHESS AUGUSTA OF SAXE–COBURG–SAALFELD
*19 March 1809*[1]

..............................................................................

Davout, though of noble birth, was lacking in charm, but he was a brave, efficient and skilful soldier, whose integrity was unquestionable. He was born at Annoux (Yonne) on 10 May 1770, the son of a lieutenant in Royal-Champagne-Cavalerie. He studied at the Military School at Auxerre, and on 29 September 1785 entered the Royal Military School of Paris, passing out on 19 February 1788, and being posted as a *sous-lieutenant* to his father's regiment[2] in garrison at Hesdin.

Davout embraced the principles of the Revolution with enthusiasm, and this got him into trouble over a toast at a regimental dinner! There was a mutiny in the corps, and he ended up in confinement in the Citadel of Arras. He sent in his papers on 15 September 1791, but a week later was elected lieutenant-colonel of the

DAVOUT
*From the portrait by Tito Marzocchi, after Claude Gautherot, engraved by*
*R. A. Muller.*

3rd Battalion of Volunteers of the Yonne.

Davout fought at Neerwinden. He tried to arrest Dumouriez (4 April 1793), ordering his men to open fire on him. He served with the Armies of the North, of Belgium and then of the Côtes de la Rochelle, being made General of Brigade (25 July 1793). He was nominated to be General of Division with the Army of the North (30 July), but wrote refusing and resigning in conformity with the decree which excluded *ci-devant* nobles from the army (29 August). He retired to his home at Ravières, but demanded to re-enter the service (11 October 1794) and was given command of a cavalry brigade in the Army of the Moselle.

In 1795 he was taken prisoner at the capitulation of Mannheim (18 September), returning to France on parole, and being exchanged whilst staying at home.

Davout was at the defence of Kehl in November 1796, and was on friendly terms with Louis-Charles-Antoine des Aix, Chevalier de Veygoux, *dit* Desaix (1768–1800), under whom he had served in 1795 in the Army of the Rhine and Moselle. At Offenburg (21 April 1797) he captured a waggon containing the correspondence of General Jean-Charles Pichegru (1761–1804). Pichegru was deported later that year.[3]

General Davout was selected for the Army of England, but Desaix presented him to Bonaparte on 22 March 1798, and instead he was attached to Headquarters for the expedition to Egypt. He fought at the Pyramids, Abukir and elsewhere. Whilst returning to France with Desaix, he was captured by the English and kept prisoner for a month at Livorno. He landed at Toulon on 6 May and was promoted General of Division (3 July 1800).

Davout was given command of the cavalry of the Army of Italy (26 August) with which he saw some action towards the end of 1800. He was made Inspector-General of Cavalry (24 July 1801), and then commander of the *grenadiers à pied* of the Consular Guard (28 November). On 29 August 1803 he was given command of the Camp of Bruges.

Davout was one of the famous promotion of 19 May 1804, and soon after became one of the four Colonel-Generals of the Imperial

Guard. In 1805 he was given the Grand Eagle of the Legion of Honour.

In the 1805 campaign Davout commanded the 3rd Corps of the Grand Army, with which he won the action at Marienzell (8 November). His Corps made a forced march from Vienna, eighty miles in fifty hours, arriving in time to play a decisive part in the battle of Austerlitz. 'Before ordering the attack', wrote Corporal Jean-Pierre Blaise of the 108th of the Line, 'Marshal Davout – who did not leave even though the cannon-balls were beginning to bother us – recalled to our minds the action at Marianzelle (*sic*).'

On 14 October 1806, while the Emperor with 96,000 men was engaging 55,000 Prussians, Davout, with but 26,000, fought the Duke of Brunswick's main body, 63,000 strong, to a standstill after six hours of stubborn defensive combat. The battle was begun in a fog and since in any case Davout's eyesight was very poor, he was at less of a disadvantage than the other generals present, whether Prussians or French. His Corps was given the honour of entering Berlin at the head of the army.

At Eylau, where he commanded the right wing, the steady pressure of Davout's 3rd Corps during the afternoon did much to swing the fortunes of that doubtful day in Napoleon's favour. He was wounded on this occasion; a severe contusion.

On 15 July the Marshal was made Governor-General of the Grand Duchy of Warsaw, and on 28 March 1808, Duke of Auerstädt, as well as being awarded pensions amounting to more than a million francs a year.

In 1809 he commanded the 3rd Corps with which he put in a most effective attack at Eckmühl. At Wagram he had a horse killed under him, but once more he played a valuable rôle driving back the Austrian left. On 15 August he was made Prince of Eckmühl.

For the next two years Davout held high commands in Germany with his H.Q. at Hamburg. In the Russian campaign of 1812 he commanded the 1st Corps. His preparations were meticulous and his command was a model both of discipline and administration. No detail was too small for his attention. He had his men's knapsacks scientifically packed so that they would hold everything they needed. His regiments were self-sufficient, and according to Ségur each had 'masons, bakers, tailors, shoemakers, gunsmiths; in short, workmen of every class. They carried everything they required with them; his army was like a colony; handmills followed. He had anticipated every want; all means of supplying them were ready.'

Before Borodino Davout, like the good infantry soldier he was, tried in vain to persuade the Emperor to make his main attack an outflanking movement, or right hook. Since the French were far abler at manœuvring than the Russians, this was much more likely to succeed than a frontal attack. But Napoleon decided upon the latter. The Marshal himself was wounded and had two horses killed in the attacks on Prince Bagration's position. Borodino proved an indecisive blood-bath and Napoleon has been much criticized, and with justice, for rejecting Davout's sound advice.

Napoleon left Moscow on 19 October 1812. His army 'looked like a caravan, a wandering nation, or rather one of those armies of antiquity returning with slaves and spoil after a great devastation' (Ségur). On 3 November Davout's Corps, which was acting as rearguard, was suddenly attacked by General Miloradovitch at Fëdorovskoye, cut off from the rest of the Grand Army and sur-rounded. Fortunately for Davout, Eugène de Beauharnais (4th Corps) divined his peril and sent two divisions to extricate him, which they did, though he suffered heavy losses. Napoleon blamed Davout for marching too slowly, and from this time entrusted the conduct of the rearguard to Marshal Ney.

On 9 November the weather broke and by mid-November Davout, who had crossed the Niemen with a corps 72,000 strong, had but 10,000 left. Napoleon now hastened his retreat but failed to inform Ney, who got cut off. Davout, whose corps was next ahead, was much abused for this, but he cannot be blamed for the vagaries of the Imperial Staff. And in fact Ney succeeded in fighting his way through.

Davout fought at the passage of the Berezina and by 27 November his corps was down to 3,000 men.

In 1813 Davout was ordered by Eugène to defend Dresden and this he did (9–19 March). But the Emperor disapproved of Eugène's dispositions, for he attached much importance to the control of the Lower Elbe, and on 30 May Davout occupied Hamburg. He won an action at Lauenburg (18 August), and then made a tenacious defence of Hamburg, which he only evacuated on 27 May 1814, after Napoleon's first abdication, when he received a formal order from King Louis XVIII.

Forbidden by the Bourbon government to appear in Paris, Davout retired to his estate at Savigny-sur-Orge and played no part in public affairs until Napoleon's return from Elba, when he was made Minister of War (20 March–8 July 1815) and a peer of France (2 June).

During the brief Waterloo campaign Davout, who was certainly superior to any of Napoleon's corps commanders, and would perhaps have been a more efficient Chief of Staff than Soult, held no active command. Napoleon wrote to him: 'I can entrust Paris to no one but you.' One is compelled to agree, for the Emperor needed a man of iron in his capital if he was to fight a campaign without looking over his shoulder all the time.

On 22 June after Waterloo Davout was charged with the defence of Paris but on that day Napoleon renounced his Imperial rights in favour of his son, the King of Rome, and though Davout had more than 100,000 men at his command, and managed to check Blücher when on 30 June he appeared before the capital, he was operating without any real political backing. On 3 July he signed at Saint-Cloud the Convention of Paris, by which the Allies occupied the capital, and the French army retired to the Loire. On 14 July he made his submission to the King, and his dismissal soon followed (27 July).

Deprived of his peerage and his pay, he was exiled to Louviers (27 December), where he was under police surveillance. However, he was reinstated on 27 August 1817, and made a peer once more on 5 March 1819. From 1819 onwards he always let himself be known by the title of Prince d'Eckmühl instead of that of Duc d'Auerstädt, which he had preferred in Imperial days. It seems that the Marshal was determined to make a clean break with the past.

Davout was married to Louise-Aimée-Julie Leclerc, sister of Lt-General Louis-Nicolas-Marin, Comte Leclerc des Essarts (1770–1820), brother of Pauline Bonaparte's first husband. This officer became a General of Brigade in 1808, and served under his brother-in-law in 1809 and 1813.

General Louis-Alexandre-Edme-François, Baron Davout (1773–1820), the Marshal's brother, rose to the rank of General of Brigade. Much of his service was spent as A.D.C. to his brother. He was made Baron in 1808.

After the Restoration Davout was not again employed in any command, and died of consumption at his hotel in the Rue Saint-Dominique, Paris, on 1 June 1823.

It may be that Davout was not quite as unpleasant as the Duchess Augusta would have us believe. To a simple soldier like Coignet he could make himself very pleasant, permitting him, because he had the Cross, to enter the Guard though he was not quite up to the height standard, and inviting him to a wolf hunt when he was on leave. In any case one can be an efficient general without being particularly pleasant, and beyond question Davout ranks with the best of Napoleon's Marshals. Since he never exercised a truly independent command, it is difficult to compare him with Masséna, Soult or Suchet. Suffice it to say that he shone both as a fighting man and an administrator. Nor was his character besmirched by any act of treachery or disloyalty.

# JEAN-BAPTISTE BESSIÈRES, DUC D'ISTRIE
## 1768–1813

Bessières lived like Bayard; he died like Turenne.

NAPOLEON

Bessières was one of the small number of the Marshals who may be numbered among Napoleon's close friends. He made his mark in command of his Guides during the first Italian campaign. He has one victory alone to his credit; Medina del Rio Seco where he routed Don Gregorio de la Cuesta, arguably the worst general of all time. But it is as a cavalry commander, rather than the commander of a force of all arms, that he deserves to be remembered.

Bessières was born at Prayssac (Lot) on 6 August 1768; and was by birth a gentleman. When the National Guard of Prayssac was formed in 1789 he was made captain of a grenadier company. He was nominated by the Department of Lot to serve as a trooper in the short-lived Constitutional Guard of the King (April 1792), and when it was disbanded in the following June he was for a short time in the battalion of Jacobins Saint-Dominique of the Paris National Guard. He served on the Pyrenees front. He held several minor staff appointments and rose to captain in the 22nd Chasseurs à Cheval (8 May 1794), before being posted to the Army of Italy. After the affair of Cremona he was chosen by Bonaparte to command his Guides (5 June 1796), and promoted *chef d'escadrons* on the battlefield of Rovereto. He distinguished himself both at Rivoli and at La Favorita and had the honour of taking to Paris the Austrian colours captured on these two occasions.

Promoted *chef de brigade*, he commanded the Guides of the

# JEAN-BAPTISTE BESSIÈRES,
## Duc d'Istrie

........................................................................

## LOUIS NICOLAS DAVOUT,
### Duc d'Auerstädt, Prince d'Eckmühl

........................................................................

General-in-Chief of the Army of the Orient (May 1798). He was at the siege of Acre and at the battle of Abukir, returning to France with his chief. During the *coup d'état* of 18 Brumaire he was commander-in-chief of the Guard of the Corps Législatif (30 November 1799), and he was then given command of the Grenadiers à Cheval de la Garde Consulaire (2 December).

Bessières fought at Marengo and was made General of Brigade and second-in-command of the Consular Guard (18 July 1800), then commander-in-chief of its cavalry (20 November 1801). He continued in high favour.

13 September 1802: General of Division.

19 May 1804: Marshal of the Empire.

14 June 1804: Grand Officer of the Legion of Honour and chief of the 3rd Cohort.

20 July 1804: Colonel-General commanding the cavalry of the Imperial Guard.

2 February 1805: Grand Eagle of the Legion of Honour. Commander of the *Couronne de Fer* (of Lombardy).

At Austerlitz he took part of the enemy artillery. He distinguished himself at Jena, and won a minor victory at Biezun (23 December 1806). He charged with the cavalry of the Guard at Eylau and served at Friedland.

He did pretty well financially, being awarded, by decree:

| Date | per annum | from |
|---|---|---|
| 30 June 1807 | 40,000 fr. | Grand Duchy of Warsaw. |
| 23 September 1807 | 20,000 fr. | Grignon and its dependencies. |
| 10 March 1808 | 53,000 fr. | Westphalia. |
| | 50,000 fr. | Hanover. |
| 29 March 1808 | 100,000 fr. | Mont de Milan. |

And more honours and decorations came his way. In addition to his Grand Eagle of the Legion of Honour he had:

the Grand Cross of St Henry of Saxony;

the Grand Cross of Christ of Portugal;

the Golden Eagle of Württemberg;

the Dukedom of Istria (28 May 1809).

BESSIÈRES
*From the painting by Edmond Hédouin, after Riesener, engraved by Charles State.*

He was in addition Ambassador to Württemberg.

On 19 March 1808 he was given command of a force, including part of the Imperial Guard, formed to observe the Pyrénées Occidentales. On 14 July there followed his victory over the Castilians and Galicians under Cuesta and Blake at Medina del Rio Seco, after which he entered Madrid with King Joseph. He commanded the 2nd Corps of the Army of Spain, but the Emperor found his movements sluggish and soon replaced him with Soult, giving him the cavalry of the army (9 November) with whom he served at Somosierra and at the capture of Madrid. He won a fight at Guadalajara and took part in the pursuit of Sir John Moore's army, being recalled to Paris on 9 March 1809.

In the Austrian campaign of that year he commanded the Reserve Cavalry. He served at Landshut, was beaten at Neumarkt, served at Ebersberg, charged at Essling, and was slightly bruised by a cannon ball at Wagram.

Made commander-in-chief of the Army of the North, in Berna-dotte's stead, he retook Flushing (1809).

On 19 January 1810 he was given command of the Imperial Guard at Paris, then for the period of the future Empress Marie-Louise's stay at Strasbourg he was made Governor of that city (19 March 1810). Made General-in-Chief of the Army of the North (15 January 1811), he served in Spain for eight months playing an undistinguished part in Masséna's failure at Fuentes de Oñoro. He arrived back in Paris on 20 September. In May 1812 he was given command of the cavalry of the Imperial Guard, at whose head he served in Russia. According to Marbot it was upon his advice that the Emperor withheld the Imperial Guard when on the evening of Borodino they might have made his victory decisive. But Napoleon must have the credit and the blame for his own decisions.

Bessières came to the Emperor's rescue when on 25 October he charged and drove off the Cossacks who were on the point of over-running Napoleon and his staff at Gorodnya.

Bessières was given command of the Imperial Guard, 10 April 1813, but he did not enjoy this appointment for long. On 1 May, on the eve of the battle of Lützen, outside the village of Rippach near Weissenfels (Saxony) he rode into the line of fire of a laid cannon and was struck by a ball which severed one of his wrists, pierced his chest and killed him instantly. It was a curious fate for so experienced a soldier, and the Emperor was much affected by the loss of one of his most loyal supporters.

Bessières is usually depicted in a uniform resembling that of the Chasseurs à Cheval of the Imperial Guard, though without a pelisse. No doubt he looked back with pleasure to the days when he had commanded Bonaparte's Guides. He seems to have been a somewhat conservative gentleman for when, in June 1804, everyone else cut off his queue he retained his – and it went half-way down his back.

Bessières was at his best commanding cavalry, but though he does not seem to have been particularly gifted as a general, he held a number of high appointments with distinction. Had he lived, one cannot imagine his siding with Marmont in 1814. Nor is it going too far to say that the Emperor could have employed him to advantage at Waterloo.

The Marshal had a young brother, Baron Bertrand Bessières (1773–1854), who was a captain in Bonaparte's Guides (1797) and in 1811 actually declined promotion to General of Division. Most unusual. He had none the less a career of some distinction and was wounded both at Borodino and at Leipzig.

# 15

# FRANÇOIS-ÉTIENNE CHRISTOPHE KELLERMANN, DUC DE VALMY

## 1735–1820

Officier très intelligent et instruit. Bon officier.

REPORT *of 1784*

Had Napoleon never lived, the name of Kellermann would still have been known to history, for his victory at Valmy is numbered among the decisive battles of the world.

Kellermann, the oldest of the Marshals, was born at Strasbourg (Bas-Rhin) on 28 May 1735; he was already 34 at the time of Napoleon's birth. He entered the *régiment de Lowendahl* in 1752 as a Volunteer Cadet, and was commissioned ensign in the *régiment Royal-Bavière* in 1754. Thus he was already an officer before the outbreak of the Seven Years War, and an ensign 31 years before the young Buonaparte became a *sous-lieutenant*.

During the Seven Years War he distinguished himself on several occasions including the Battle of Bergen (13 April 1759) when the Duc de Broglie repulsed Ferdinand of Brunswick. In 1771 he served in Poland in a corps of volunteers under the Baron de Vioménil, and trained the cavalry of the Cracow area. On 13 July 1771 he was made chevalier of Saint-Louis.

Kellermann served in many different regiments and on 15 February 1784, when he was 48, he was promoted *Mestre de Camp en Second* of the senior regiment of Hussars, that entitled *Colonel Général*. On 9 March he was promoted *Maréchal de Camp*, and it may therefore be said that he was well on the road to high rank before the Revolution. He continued to prosper. On 7 March 1792

134

KELLERMANN
*From the painting by Georges Rouget, engraved by Henry Wolf.*

he became Commander of Saint-Louis, on 20 March a lieutenant-general; on 1 October he replaced Marshal Count Luckner in command of the Army of the Centre (later of the Moselle). Though subordinate to Dumouriez, he was the real victor of Valmy. On his success he drove back the Prussians and took Longwy and Verdun.

During the years that followed, Kellermann suffered the usual tribulations of a French Revolutionary general. Despite his triumph he was deprived of his command on 5 November 1792. Given the Army of the Alps (11 November), he survived there until 25 April 1793. Named commander-in-chief of the Armies of the Alps and of Italy (20 May 1793), he besieged Lyons and drove the enemy from Savoy, only to be dismissed and imprisoned in the Abbaye.

Reinstated on 15 January 1795, Kellermann was sent again to the Alps and Italy (3 March). He gave up command in Italy (28 September), remaining in command of the Army of the Alps until it was done away with on 13 September 1797. Thereafter he held a number of high commands of secondary importance, inspector-general of this and that, commander of reserve corps, and so on. He became a senator (24 December 1799) and later President of the Senate. Made Marshal of the Empire in 1804, and given the Grand Cross of the Legion of Honour in 1805, he became Duke of Valmy on 3 June 1808. Despite his advanced years Napoleon employed him as late as 20 January 1813 in command of the Corps of Observation on the Rhine.

After the first abdication Kellermann was the King's Commissioner in the 3rd Military Division (May 1814), and was made a peer of France (4 June)[1] and Governor of the 5th Military Division at his native Strasbourg where he had first seen the light seventy-nine years before. On 23 August 1814 the Grand Cross of Saint-Louis was bestowed upon him. Nevertheless Napoleon also made him a peer during the Hundred Days (2 June 1815), but the old soldier kept aloof. Perhaps at heart he felt more at home under the Bourbons he had served in his youth, rather than under the Emperor who had recognized the greatness of a victory that he had won, not so much for the Republic as for *la France*!

# 16

# FRANÇOIS-JOSEPH LEFEBVRE, DUC DE DANTZIG

## 1755–1820

A sergeant of the Gardes Françaises.

Born at Rouffach (Haut-Rhin) on 25 October 1755, Lefebvre enlisted as a soldier in the Gardes Françaises (10 September 1773) and by 1782 was a sergeant. He was transferred to a grenadier company and on 9 April 1788 became senior sergeant. On 12 July 1789 he managed to rescue some of his officers who were being ill-treated by the mob. He was promoted lieutenant and was instructor to the battalion of the Filles Saint-Thomas in the National Guard of Paris (1 September 1789), and was wounded while protecting the Royal Family on its return to the Tuileries after its attempt to depart for Saint-Cloud, and in assisting the flight of the aunts of Louis XVI. On 1 January 1792 he was promoted captain in the 13th light infantry battalion, and served in the Army of the Centre (later of the Moselle), 1792–3. On 2 December 1793 he was promoted General of Brigade, and saw a good deal of fighting, notably the battle of Fleurus. He won a minor victory at Bracquignies (1 July 1794), and was given command of the 2nd Division of the Army on 7 August 1794. He served with credit under Kléber in 1795 and 1796. For a few months, after the death of Hoche, he actually commanded the celebrated Army of the Sambre-et-Meuse (19 September–14 December 1797). Although he was to the fore in a score of long forgotten fights he only seems to have been wounded once, hit in the left arm by a

musket ball in a combat at Pfallendorf (21 March 1799). This led
to his return to Paris, where he was given command of the 17th
Military Division, and was, therefore, well-placed to play an
important rôle in the *coup d'état* of 18 Brumaire. He became a
senator in April 1800 and later the President of the Senate.

On 19 May 1804 he was made a Marshal of the Empire, one of
the four made, as it were, *honoris causa*. But there was life in the
old dog yet and unlike the other three he played the part of a
fighting general under the Empire. On 2 February 1805 he was
invested with the Grand Eagle of the Legion of Honour.

On 11 September 1806 he took Mortier's place as commander
of the 5th Corps of the Grand Army, and on 5 October he took
command of the infantry of the Imperial Guard – not a bad appointment for a former sergeant of the Gardes Françaises.

He served at Jena, and was given command of the 10th Corps
for the siege of Danzig (23 January 1807), though the Emperor
had taken the kindly precaution of seeing that the old foot soldier
had competent engineers to supervise the technical side of the
siege. The city capitulated on 24 May 1807, and Lefebvre was the
first of the Marshals to be made a duke.

Lefebvre next saw active service in Spain, in command of the
4th Corps. He did rather well. He defeated the Marquis de la
Romaña at Durango (31 October 1808), took Santander, won the
battle of Guenes against Blake (7 November) and played a part in
the battle of Espinosa (10 November).

In the Austrian campaign of 1809 Lefebvre was active once
more. Commanding the 7th (Bavarian) Corps, he won a minor
victory at Arnhofen (19 April) and fought at Eckmühl. In command
of the Army of the Tirol (May–October) he defeated General
Jellachich and took Innsbruck.

Lefebvre commanded the infantry of the Old Guard during the
Russian campaign and was at the battle of Borodino. He was active
in trying to sort out the stragglers from every unit and formation
at the bridges of the Berezina. He was recalled to Paris on 11
January 1813, but saw active service again in the campaign of
France. He was at Champaubert and Montmirail, and particularly

LEFEBVRE
*Sketch by Eric Pape from a contemporary portrait.*

distinguished himself at Montereau, where at the head of the Emperor's staff he seized the vital bridge. Captain Coignet describes the scene as the intrepid marshal led the charge.

'As we rode over the bridge, a large gap in it was no obstacle to us, on account of the speed with which we came. Our horses flew! ... At the end of the bridge, which is long, there is a street to the left. This faubourg being blocked up with the wagons belonging to the rearguard, we had to fight our way through with our sabres. We swept everything before us. Those who escaped our fury did so by dragging themselves under the wagons. Our marshal fought so hard that he foamed at the mouth.' He was 59.

This was probably Lefebvre's last fight. Soon afterwards he made one of the group of marshals that brought about the first abdication of Napoleon. When the Emperor returned in 1815 he played no part in affairs, pleading, not without reason, that he was too old.

Lefebvre married Catherine Hubscher, the legendary 'Madame Sans Gêne'.

It is said of Lefebvre that on one occasion some young man envied his handsome house and its good appointments, to be told that if he would let the Marshal have sixty shots at him in the garden, and survived, he could have the lot. ... The Marshal reckoned that he had been missed by many more shots, and at shorter range, before he became master of these coveted possessions.

# 17

# CATHERINE-DOMINIQUE, MARQUIS DE PÉRIGNON

## 1754–1818

### The Royalist

Pérignon was one of the four honorary Marshals of the 1804 creation. Though he held several important commands under the Empire, he fought in none of the great Napoleonic battles: his fighting record belongs to the period of the Revolutionary Wars. In his last years his conduct was consistently Royalist.

Born at Grenade (Haute-Garonne) on 31 May 1754, he served for a few years in the army of the Old Régime. He was commissioned (6 July 1780) as *sous-lieutenant* in the garrison battalion of the *Régiment de Lyonnais*, passing (18 August 1782) to the *Grenadiers Royaux de Quercy*. He was also A.D.C. to Maréchal de Camp le Comte de Preissac who became a Lt-General on 1 January 1784. But by this time, it seems, Pérignon had retired, and it was not until July 1789 that he took up arms once more. This time it was as lieutenant-colonel of the National Guard of Montech (Haute-Garonne), a unit dissolved on 30 March 1791.

Pérignon was evidently quite a figure in his own department; he was justice of the peace (1790) and deputy to the Legislative Assembly (1791). Made lieutenant-colonel of the infantry of the *Légion des Pyrénées*, he saw a good deal of fighting and rose rapidly to the rank of General of Division (confirmed 23 December 1793). After some successes including the capture of Rosas (3 February 1795), he was beaten at Bàscara (6 May) and replaced by General Schérer (30 May). Nevertheless he was nominated as commander-in-chief of the Coasts of Brest and Cherbourg (13 November), but instead of taking up this command he went as Ambassador to

Spain (26 November 1795–21 December 1797). He was put on the retired list on 24 August 1798, but almost immediately re-employed with the Army of Italy (14 October). He was seriously wounded in the head, forearm and other places and taken prisoner at Novi, only returning to France at the end of 1800. On 5 January 1801 he was given command of the 10th Military Division at Toulouse, but he did not hold it for long, for on 12 April he became a senator and was pensioned on 18 November. His experience in the 1790s led to his being appointed commissioner extraordinary to regulate the frontiers between France and Spain (11 September 1802). On 27 October he was made Vice-President of the Senate. He was made a Marshal of the Empire in 1804, and invested with the Grand Eagle of the Legion of Honour in 1805.

Further service in Italy followed. He was appointed Governor-General of the States of Parma and Plasencia, 18 September 1806; on 23 July 1808 he became Governor of Naples, commanding under King Joachim (Murat) the French troops stationed in that kingdom, posts held under King Joseph by Marshal Jourdan. This brought him reward for on 9 October he was made Grand Dignitary of the Order of the Two Sicilies. He was already (19 March 1808) a Count of the Empire with two *dotations* of 20,000 fr. each on the reserved domains of Westphalia and Hanover. He was retired on 27 March 1813, but re-employed immediately after the Emperor's first abdication when the Comte d'Artois made him the King's extraordinary commissioner in the 1st Military Division. Next he was President of the Commission appointed to examine the qualifications of former officers. For these services (31 May–10 October 1814) he was made a chevalier of Saint-Louis (1 June) and a peer of France (4 June). On 28 March 1815 the Duc d'Angoulême provisionally made him Governor of Toulouse; however, he did not take up the appointment but retired to his estate at Montech. On 10 April, with the Emperor restored, his name was struck from the list of Marshals; it was restored on 24 July.

Under Louis XVIII he was Governor of the 1st Military Division (10 January 1816), and was made Commander of Saint-Louis (3 May 1816); awarded the Grand Cross of that order (24

August); and created Marquis (31 August 1817). He was also one
of the peers who voted for the execution of Marshal Ney.

# 18

# JEAN-MATHIEU-PHILIBERT, COMTE SÉRURIER

## 1742–1819

A veteran of the Seven Years War.

Sérurier was Governor of Les Invalides throughout the First Empire.

Born at Laon (Aisne) on 8 December 1742, Sérurier entered the army as a Lieutenant in the Laon Militia battalion on 25 March 1755. On 1 October 1759 he became an ensign in the *régiment d'infanterie d'Aumont*, with whom he campaigned in Germany, being wounded in the jaw by a musket shot at the battle of Warburg (31 July 1760). Promoted lieutenant (25 April 1762), he took part in the Portuguese expedition of June–November that year. He transferred to *Beauce-infanterie*, where he was instructor (1763–9). He took part in the Corsican expedition of 1770–1, commanding a detachment of chasseurs. He became a chevalier of Saint-Louis (30 July 1781) and on 17 March 1789 was promoted major of *Médoc-infanterie*, which became the 91st of the Line in 1791. He was promoted lieutenant-colonel (1 January 1791). While in garrison at Perpignan, his soldiers revolted and seized the regimental colours and chest. On 7 August 1792 he was made colonel of the 70th of the Line, but on 10 October he was deprived of his rank and arrested as a suspected Royalist. He owed his reinstatement to the influence of Barras, to whom Napoleon himself was to owe his early advancement. Sérurier distinguished himself in a combat at Utelle (28 February 1793) and was made provisional general of brigade by the Representatives of the People with the Army of Italy, who included Barras, on 25 June 1793, and on 22 December

SÉRURIER
*From the painting by Jean-Louis Laneuville.*

1794 he was promoted provisional General of Division, this rank being confirmed by the Committee of Public Safety on 13 June 1795. Thanks to a series of successes, his reputation stood high when Bonaparte arrived to take command of the Army of Italy. Under his orders he won the battle of Mondovi. He was entrusted with the blockade and siege of Mantua (4 June–1 August, and 21 December–2 February). He defeated General Provera at La Favorita and received the capitulation of Mantua (2 February 1797). Sérurier's health had suffered during these operations, probably from malaria, and on 3 June Bonaparte gave him the duty of carrying twenty-two captured colours to the Directory. However, he returned to Italy and was Governor of Venice from 18 October 1797 to 18 January 1798, when he evacuated that city.

Sérurier distinguished himself at Pastrengo (26 March 1799), but was compelled to capitulate at Verderio after an energetic resistance.

Released on parole by Suvorov, Sérurier played his part in the *coup* of 18 Brumaire, as commandant of the reserve at Point du Jour (10 November 1799), though he did not intervene at Saint-Cloud, when Bonaparte was in danger. He was retired on 13 August 1801, and became Vice-President of the Senate (22 December 1802). In 1803 he was President of the Commission appointed to decide upon the frontiers between France and Liguria.

On 23 April 1804 he was made Governor of Les Invalides, a very appropriate choice seeing that he had been a commissioned officer for forty-six years, and had fought in the Seven Years War.

On 19 May 1804 he was one of the four made honorary Marshals of the Empire. Other honours came his way: Grand Eagle of the Legion of Honour (1805) and Grand Cordon of the Iron Crown. He was created Count (1808), and received monetary awards amounting to 40,000 fr. a year.

He commanded the National Guard of Paris (3 September 1809) and was President of the Court of Inquiry which examined the circumstances in which General Charles-Mathieu-Isidore Decaen (1769–1832) had surrendered the Ile de France (3 December 1810).

On 31 March 1814, when the Allies were about to enter Paris, Sérurier had 1,417 captured colours broken and burnt in the Grande Cour (Cour d'Honneur) des Invalides. The pensioners, many of whom had fought that day under Marshal Moncey at the Barrière de Clichy, were all assembled, and when the holocaust was at its height the white-haired veteran Marshal with his own hand cast into the flames the sword and sash of King Frederick the Great of Prussia, spoils of the 1806 campaign. Anyone with a love for things military must regret the proud gesture!

The Bourbons made Sérurier a peer of France (4 June 1814), as did Napoleon on his return from Elba (2 June 1815), and as a peer he was among those who voted for the execution of Ney.

On 27 December 1815 he was replaced as Governor of Les Invalides by an old Royalist officer. This was the Duc de Coigny (1737–1821) who received his marshal's baton at the age of 79! Sérurier received a pension of 20,000 fr. a year and the Grand Cross of Saint-Louis (30 September 1818). He was put back on the active list as a Marshal of France on 1 January 1819 but died in Paris on 21 December following and was interred at Père Lachaise. In 1847 his body was exhumed and removed to Les Invalides.

Chandler, in *The Campaigns of Napoleon*, describes him, somewhat harshly: 'He was a methodical worker and severe disciplinarian, somewhat out of place in this citizen army [of 1796], and had few claims to military distinction; an air of aristocratic nostalgia lingered around this *ci-devant* nobleman.'[1]

# 19

# CLAUDE VICTOR-PERRIN, DIT VICTOR, DUC DE BELLUNE
## 1764–1841

Beau Soleil.
*The Nickname of Marshal Victor*

Perrin, or Victor as he called himself, was born at Lamarche (Vosges) on 7 December 1764, son of a notary, and enlisted as a drummer in the Artillery Regiment of Grenoble on 16 October 1781, when he was nearly 17. In 1791 he served as a grenadier in the National Guard of Valence, before enlisting (12 October) in the 3rd battalion of Volunteers of the Drôme. Previous experience, even as a drummer boy, stood a man in good stead in the early days of the Armies of the First Republic. *Adjudant sous-officier* (21 February 1792) Victor was captain and adjutant-major of the 5th battalion of Volunteers of the Bouches du Rhône (4 August) and lieutenant-colonel of the same unit on 15 September. From 1792 to 1793 he served with the Army of Italy, distinguishing himself at the combat of Coaraze and the siege of Toulon, and being nominated provisional *chef de brigade* by the Representatives of the People with the Army operating against the insurgents in the South (2 October 1793). He was to the fore once again in the attack on Mont Faron (1 December), and given command of a division.

Victor was hit and gravely wounded by a burst of grapeshot in the lower stomach at the storming of the British redoubt known as Little Gibraltar (17 December 1793), but made provisional General of Brigade three days later.

Victor went next to the Army of the Pyrénées-Orientales (1

VICTOR
*Drawing by Eric Pape from the portrait by Antoine-Jean Gros.*

January 1794) where he served under Pérignon among others. He was at the battles of Saint-Laurent de la Mouga (13 August) and of the Montagne Noire (17–20 November) as well as the siege of Rosas (24 November–3 February 1795). His promotion to General of Brigade was confirmed by the Committee of Public Safety (13 June 1795).

Posted to Masséna's division of the Army of Italy in 1795, he saw a great deal of service there during the next five years. He fought at Borghetto (3 October), at Loano (23–5 November), at

149

Dego (14–15 April 1796) and Roveredo; was wounded at San Giorgio (15 September); fought at Rivoli and La Favorita and on 18 January 1797 was made a provisional General of Division by Bonaparte, being confirmed in this rank by the Executive Directory on 10 March 1797. Meanwhile he had beaten the Papal forces on the River Senio, and captured Ancona (9 February).

After a brief spell with the Army of England under Kléber (12 January 1798), his request to be sent back to Italy was granted (3 May). In 1799 he saw a good deal of fighting and was wounded at the battle of the Trebbia. In 1800 he served at Montebello and distinguished himself at Marengo, for which he received a sabre of honour (6 July).

Victor held high commands in Holland from 25 July 1800 to 5 February 1804, and was nominated Captain-General of Louisiana on 9 August 1802, though he did not go there. He was made Minister Plenipotentiary in Denmark on 19 February 1805. On 6 March he was awarded the Grand Eagle of the Legion of Honour.

In the 1806 campaign Victor was Chief of Staff to Marshal Lannes (7 October), serving at Saalfeld and Jena and signing the capitulation of Spandau (25 October). He fought at Pultusk and was then given command of Dombrowski's Polish Division (4 January 1807) and the 10th Corps (5 January), but on his way to Stettin had the misfortune to fall into the hands of 25 Prussian chasseurs under the celebrated partisan, Major Schill, on 20 January. He was, however, exchanged on 8 March, and given charge of the siege of Graudenz (23 May), and then of the 1st Corps of the Grand Army, in place of Bernadotte, on 6 June. He served at Friedland. The Marshal's baton followed on 13 July.

Victor was made Governor of Prussia and of Berlin (9 August) and between 30 June 1807 and 29 March 1808 received five pensions amounting in all to 157,939 fr. a year.

On 10 September 1808 Victor was made a Duke. Because of his handsome, open countenance he was nicknamed 'Beau-Soleil',[1] and one of Napoleon's sisters maliciously suggested that he be called 'Bellune'. The thing was done, but when the reason came to light neither the Emperor nor the Marshal appreciated the joke.

Three days earlier Victor had been given command of the 1st Corps of the Army of Spain, with which he defeated Blake at Espinosa (10–11 November). He was at Somosierra and the capture of Madrid. In 1809 he defeated the Spaniards at the battles of Ucles (13 January) and Medellín (28 March) and beat Don Gregorio de la Cuesta at Alcabon (26 July). But pitted against the British, he did not do so well. At Talavera, though he and Jourdan outnumbered Wellesley, they were defeated with fairly severe losses.

Victor took part in the invasion of Andalusia and again suffered defeat at the hands of a British general when he attacked Sir Thomas Graham at Barrosa (or Chiclana as the French call it) on 5 March 1811. Once more the French had outnumbered the Anglo-Spanish army opposed to them.

The Marshal was authorized to return to France (4 December) and gave up his command on 9 February 1812. But he was soon given the 9th (Reserve) Corps of the Grand Army (3 April) which he led in Russia. He did rather well in 1812, especially when commanding the rearguard at the passage of the Berezina (27–8 November).

In 1813 Victor saw a good deal of action, and was in the battles of Dresden and Leipzig. During the campaign of France, after serving at Saint-Dizier, Brienne and La Rothière, he was deprived of his command for his tardy appearance at Montereau, though he was immediately given two provisional divisions of the Young Guard (18 February). His campaigning days were, however, numbered for he was wounded by a musket shot at Craonne and saw no further action.

The Bourbon Government made him Governor of the 2nd Military Division at Mézières, and on the return of Napoleon he attempted in vain to organize resistance against him at Châlons-sur-Marne (16 March 1815). He then went to Ghent and joined King Louis XVIII, with whom he returned to Paris on 8 July. In the meanwhile Napoleon had struck his name from the list of Marshals (10 April).

Victor was made a peer of France (17 August), and one of four major-generals of the Royal Guard (8 September). He had the bad taste to vote for the death of Marshal Ney; and was President of the Commission set up to examine the services of officers during the Hundred Days (12 October). From 14 December 1821 to 19 October 1823 he was Minister of War, and thereafter was a Minister of State and a Member of the Privy Council (28 October 1822), as well as a member of the *conseil supérieur de la guerre* (1 February 1828–1 August 1830).

Victor was a knight of the Golden Fleece, held the Grand Cross of the Order of Charles III of Spain, and was a commander of Christ of Portugal. He was given the Grand Cross of Saint-Louis (24 August 1820) and made a *chevalier commandeur du Saint-Esprit* (30 September 1820): not too bad for one who had risen from the corps of drums, though as the son of a lawyer his education was probably better than that of some of his colleagues – Augereau and Ney, for example. As a commander he may perhaps be termed *Bon général ordinaire*. He could make short work of Blake or Cuesta, but was no match for Wellesley or Graham.

Victor seems to have been well enough treated by Napoleon. Promotion, honours and money all came his way, but from the time of the first abdication he threw in his lot whole-heartedly with the Royal family whose army he had joined thirty-three years ago. Perhaps the old Revolutionary merely wished to retain his title, his riches and his estate: perhaps he felt a nostalgia for the days of his youth and that ordered world, before everyone talked of *Les Droits de l'Homme* and he and his like ventured to send Kings and Queens – and Marshals – to the guillotine. When in 1840 the body of Napoleon was brought to the Invalides Victor was still alive, but he avoided the ceremony. He died in Paris on 1 March 1841.

# 20

# JACQUES-ÉTIENNE-JOSEPH-ALEXANDRE MACDONALD, DUC DE TARENTE

## 1765–1840

C'est sur le champ de bataille de votre gloire, où je vous dois une grande partie de cette journée d'hier, que je vous fais maréchal de France; il y a longtemps que vous le méritiez.[1]

NAPOLEON TO MACDONALD
*on 7 July 1809, the day after the battle of Wagram*

..................................................................................

Macdonald was a useful corps commander and a man of strong and upright character. He was an able administrator as well as a good tactician.

He was born, the son of a Scots Jacobite exile, at Sedan (Ardennes) on 17 November 1765 and joined the *Légion Irlandaise* in 1784. He served for a time as a lieutenant in the *Légion de Maillebois* in the Dutch service (1 April 1785), and then entered the Regiment of Dillon as a volunteer (12 July 1786). When the Revolution came he was a *sous-lieutenant*.

Macdonald was A.D.C., successively, to General Pierre de Ruel de Beurnonville[2] (1752–1821) and to General Charles-François du Périer, *dit* Dumouriez (1739–1823) and served at Jemappes. He was promoted lieutenant-colonel in the 14th Infantry (12 November) and General of Brigade with the Army of the North (27 August 1793).

Macdonald was in the battle of Tourcoing, where the Prince of Saxe-Coburg and the Duke of York, trying to be too clever by

153

half, failed to concentrate their six converging columns at the right time and place. He was at Hondschoote and was promoted General of Division (28 November 1794).

After some service in Holland (1795–6 and 1798) and with the Army of the *Sambre-et-Meuse* and the Army of the North, he was posted to Italy and made Governor of Rome (19 November 1798). He fell out with General Jean-Étienne Vachier, *dit* Championnet (1762–1800) and was to be sent to the Army of Mayence, but the wheel turned and on 13 February 1799 he found himself nominated commander-in-chief of the Army of Naples in Championnet's stead. He won the combat at Modena on 12 June when he was wounded. After evacuating the kingdom of Naples he was defeated on the Trebbia.

Macdonald was sent to the Army of the Rhine on 7 December 1799 as second-in-command to General Jean-Victor Moreau (1736–1813) and in 1804 he was to be disgraced for defending Moreau from the charge of treason. But before that he was Minister Plenipotentiary to Denmark (April 1801–January 1802).

Macdonald was employed again in 1807 when he was authorized to join the Neapolitan service (28 February). In 1809 he commanded a corps under Prince Eugène and was wounded at the battle of the Piave (8 May). At Wagram his great column broke the Austrian centre and decided the fate of the day. Napoleon, who had mistrusted him, took him by the hand saying 'Come, let us be friends from now on', and gave him the coveted baton (12 July), which he thoroughly deserved. He was the only one of the twenty-six to be promoted on the battlefield.

The Emperor was nothing if not whole-hearted. Soon the Grand Eagle of the Legion of Honour adorned the new Marshal's breast (14 August). An annuity of 60,000 fr. from Naples followed, and on 9 December 1809 the Marshal was made Duke of Tarentum.

Macdonald had a tour in Catalonia (24 April 1810–20 September 1811) without any particular disasters or triumphs. He then commanded the 10th Corps of the Grand Army in Russia, where he conducted the unsuccessful siege of Riga (August–December 1812).

In 1813 Macdonald was given command of the 11th Corps (10

MACDONALD
*From the painting by Jacques-Louis David. engraved by E. H. Delorme.*

April) with which he won an action at Merseburg (29 April). He commanded Napoleon's right wing at Lützen, had another success at Bischofswerda (12 May), and again led the right of the Grand Army at Bautzen. This good record was broken when he was defeated by Blücher on the Katzbach (26 August) and his corps routed. At Leipzig the Marshal narrowly escaped capture whilst crossing the River Elster under fire. He fought at Hanau.

In November 1813 Macdonald was charged with the defence of the Lower Rhine, but in January 1814 he was compelled to retreat from Cologne on Châlons-sur-Marne, which he evacuated on 4 February. He fought at Mormant (17 February), and La Ferté-sur-Aube (28 February). After evacuating Troyes (4 March), he was in action at Nogent-sur-Seine and Provins (17 March), then at Saint-Dizier (26 March).

After the fall of Paris Ney, supported by Lefebvre, Moncey and Macdonald, pressed Napoleon to come to terms with the Allies (4 April). 'We have decided to make an end of this,' he told the Emperor. Napoleon abdicated in favour of his son, and appointed Ney and Macdonald to take the document to the Tsar. They picked up Marmont on the way. He was embarrassed. Well he might be. His corps was already within the allied lines.

'I would give an arm if this had not happened,' said Marmont.

'An arm? Say rather your head, sir', retorted Macdonald.

The Marshal was made a peer of France (4 June 1814), Governor of the 21st Military Division at Bourges (21 June). In 1815 he escorted Louis XVIII to the frontier; then, returning to Paris, played no part in public affairs until after Waterloo. As he had not declared for Napoleon in 1815 he was *persona grata* with the Bourbons when they returned, and was given command of the Army of the Loire, which it was his task to disband. He exercised his authority with great moderation as is evident from the memoirs of Coignet, an ardent Bonapartist.

In his old age Macdonald wrote his memoirs, which are of great interest, and visited his relations in Scotland. He died at the Château de Courcelles-le-Roi (Loiret) on 7 September 1840.

In 1814 Napoleon, abandoned by many of his oldest friends, was very moved when Macdonald, like Moncey and Mortier, went to salute him for a last time before he left for Elba. 'Duke of Tarentum,' said the Emperor, 'I could not be more touched than I am by your conduct and devotion. . . . You, who owe me nothing, have remained true to me.'

# NICOLAS-CHARLES OUDINOT, DUC DE REGGIO

## 1767–1847

> Père des Grenadiers.
>
> *The nickname of Marshal Oudinot*

With more than a score[1] of wounds Oudinot was certainly Napoleon's most battered Marshal, though it did not prevent his living to the age of 80.

Oudinot was born at Bar-le-Duc (Meuse) on 25 April 1767, the son of a brewer. He enlisted voluntarily in the *Régiment de Médoc Infanterie* on 2 June 1784 and served until 30 April 1787. On 14 July 1789 he became captain of a troop of cavalry, and on 7 November 1790 *chef de légion* of the National Guard of the Meuse. On 6 September 1791 he was promoted lieutenant-colonel of the Volunteers of the Meuse. From 1792 to 1794 he served with the Armies of the Rhine and of the Moselle.

Oudinot was hit for the first time at Haguenau (17 December 1793) – a musket shot in the head. He became a provisional General of Brigade on 14 June 1794, and had a leg broken by a bullet at Trèves (8 August), where he was commandant from 23 August 1794 to 7 September 1795. His new rank was confirmed by the Committee of Public Safety on 13 June 1795.

His quota of wounds increased rapidly when he was captured at Neckarau after receiving five sabre cuts and a musket shot (18 October). Exchanged on 7 January 1796, he was commanding a cavalry brigade when on 11 September he received another four sabre cuts and a shot through the thigh near the bridge of Ingolstadt.

After various ups and downs Oudinot was made General of Division on 12 April 1799, and collected another shot, in the chest this time, at Rosenberg at the defence of the entrenched camp of Zürich (4 June 1799). He became Chief of Staff of the Army of the Danube and Switzerland in place of Suchet (25 July), but this did not make life any safer for him. He was hit in the shoulder-blade at Schwyz (14 August) and shot full in the chest at Zürich (25 September), which did not prevent his being in action at Adelfingen on 7 October.

Oudinot went with Masséna to the Army of Italy and took part in his defence of Genoa. He was then Chief of Staff to Brune (22 August 1800) and distinguished himself at the passage of the Mincio at Monzembano (26 December).

On 5 February 1805 Oudinot was given command of the Reserve of Grenadiers at Arras, replacing Junot, and on 6 March he was awarded the Grand Eagle of the Legion of Honour.

In the 1805 campaign Oudinot's Grenadiers were the 1st Division of Lannes's (5th) Corps, but their commander was laid low early on when a musket ball traversed his thigh at Hollabrunn (16 November). He did not see action again until Ostrolenka (16 February 1807). He was with Lefebvre at the siege of Danzig (March) and was left in command there (24 May). His next injury was a broken leg sustained when his horse fell while he was visiting a fort there. This did not prevent his serving at Friedland.

Oudinot did well in the matter of annuities and decorations. At one time he was worth more than 185,000 francs a year over and above his pay and allowances, and by 1810 had at least eight orders besides his Grand Eagle. On 2 July 1808 he was made a Count of the Empire and on 14 April 1810 Duke of Reggio.

Wounds too continued to come his way. At Essling it was another sabre cut. At Wagram a bullet nearly detached one ear, and the Grenadier Pils did a delightful sketch of him sitting nonchalantly on the battlefield while a surgeon stitched it on again.

Oudinot was promoted Marshal on 12 July 1809.

He commanded the 2nd Corps in Russia and won the battle of Polotsk, where he was seriously wounded by a grapeshot in the

OUDINOT
*From the painting by Robert Lefevre, engraved by Henry Wolf.*

····················································································

## AUGUSTE-FRÉDÉRIC-LOUIS VIESSE DE MARMONT,
Duc de Raguse

····················································································

PRINCE JOSEF ANTON PONIATOWSKI

shoulder, and had to hand over to Gouvion Saint-Cyr (18 August).
He resumed command in October only to be wounded once more
at the passage of the Berezina – a musket ball this time (28 November). Two days later he was besieged by the Russians in a house
and damaged again (30 November).

Oudinot survived the 1813 campaign unscathed, though he
fought at Bautzen and Leipzig and was defeated by Bernadotte at
Grossbeeren (23 August). The campaign of France, however,
brought him new scars. At Brienne a cannon-ball grazed both
his thighs; he was in action three days later at La Rothière. At
Arcis-sur-Aube he was struck full in the chest by a musket ball –
as he had been nearly fifteen years earlier at Zurich: but this time
he had the Grand Eagle of the Legion of Honour and its plaque
deadened the blow.

The Bourbons gave Oudinot command of the *Corps Royal des
Grenadiers* (20 May), made him a commander of Saint-Louis (2
June) and a peer of France (4 June). He was made governor of the
3rd Military Division (Metz).

When Napoleon returned from Elba he attempted to keep his
troops true to the King, but in vain. Although he was present at
the Champ de Mai (1 June), he was unemployed during the
Hundred Days, and so on the return of the Bourbons continued
his career. He even saw one more campaign, for he led the 1st
Corps in the Spanish campaign of 1823, and was for a time Governor
of Madrid. In 1839 he became Grand Chancellor of the Légion
d'Honneur, and in 1842 Governor of the Hôtel des Invalides where
he died on 13 September 1847, full of years, and the honour due
to a straight-forward fighting man, who had been a splendid
divisional commander and, under the eye of the Emperor, a
respectable commander of a corps.

It is said that a favourite pastime of his after dinner was to
shoot out candles with his pistols.

# 22

# AUGUSTE-FRÉDÉRIC-LOUIS VIESSE DE MARMONT, DUC DE RAGUSE

## 1774–1852

Marmont has struck me the final blow! Unhappy man, I loved him!
NAPOLEON
*1814*

...........................................................................

In the eyes of Napoleon's admirers the name of Judas ranks higher than that of Marmont: the verb *raguser*, derived from his title, is *to betray*.

Marmont, the youngest of the Marshals, was born at Châtillon-sur-Seine (Côte-d'Or) on 20 July 1774, and joined the garrison battalion of Chartres on 6 July 1790, when he was not quite 16. He became cadet *sous-lieutenant* at the Artillery School of Chalons (1 March 1792) and passed out as a *lieutenant en 2ᵉ* in the 1st Foot Artillery (formerly La Fère) on 1 September 1792. After service with the Army of the Alps, he was at the siege of Toulon, and was promoted captain on 12 November 1793, when he was only 19. Marmont served under Desaix with the Army of the Rhine and distinguished himself at Mayence (29 October 1795). On 3 February 1796 he became an A.D.C. to Bonaparte with the Army of the Interior, was promoted *chef de bataillon* of Artillery (8 February), and followed his general to Italy (27 March). After fighting at Cherasco and Lodi he became senior A.D.C. to Bonaparte, served at Castiglione and at the siege of Mantua, before being given the honour of taking 22 captured colours to the Directory (4 October). When Marmont was still only 22, his general, who was himself 27, made him provisional *chef de brigade*

163

of the 2nd Regiment of Horse Artillery whilst retaining him as his
chief A.D.C. The Executive Directory confirmed his new rank on
1 January 1797.

Marmont went with Bonaparte to the Army of the Orient (May
1798). At Malta he seized the banner of the Order of the Knights
of St John (10 June 1798), and was made provisional General of
Brigade the same day. He was given a light infantry brigade, in
General Bon's Division (23 June) with which he served at the
capture of Alexandria and the battle of the Pyramids. He was
one of the few selected to return to France with Bonaparte (22
August 1799), and took part in the *coup* of 18 Brumaire. Soon after
he was made a Councillor of State (*section de la guerre*).

Marmont commanded the artillery at Marengo, and was promoted General of Division (9 September 1800), when he was just
26! He served at the passages of the Mincio (26 December), the
Adige and the Brenta, and signed the armistice of Treviso,
16 January 1801.

On 16 September 1802 Marmont was made chief inspector-
general of artillery and in the following year (14 June 1803)
commandant-in-chief of the artillery of the six camps of the
Grand Army.

During the eight years in which Marmont had served with
Bonaparte he had been advanced from captain to general, and
had been shown every mark of favour. None the less he was unquestionably a well-educated officer with real talent, and it may be
surmised that it was a blow to his self-esteem when he did not
find his name among those of the Marshals of the 1804 creation.
It must have seemed to him that he had other claims than the
Emperor's friendship, whereas Bessières, for example, owed his
baton merely to the fact that he had commanded Bonaparte's
guides.

Marmont was made Colonel-General of Hussars and Chasseurs
on 1 February 1805, and Grand Eagle of the Legion of Honour
next day. It is in the uniform of that appointment that he appears
in the Plates. On 30 August Napoleon gave him command of the
2nd Corps of the Grand Army. He contributed to the victory at

**MARMONT**
*From the painting by Jean-Baptiste-Paulin Guérin, engraved by T. Johnson.*

Ulm, and won the action at Weyer (3 November) before being sent to command the 1st Corps of the Army of Italy (23 December). He was made Governor-General of Dalmatia (7 July 1806) and compelled the Russian, Admiral Siniavin, to abandon the siege of Ragusa. He was an energetic administrator, a diligent builder of roads and schools. He was made Duke of Ragusa on 15 April 1808.

In 1809 Marmont commanded the 11th Corps of the Grand Army. Wounded at Gradschatz, Croatia, on 17 May, he nevertheless won the action at Göspich three days later. He captured Fiume on 28 May, took part in the capture of Graz, and was in reserve at Wagram. He won the battle of Znaim on 9 July, and was given his baton on 12 July. In the army it was said that he owed this promotion to Napoleon's friendship. But in fact his record, both as a commander and as an administrator, compares well with those of many of his fellow Marshals.

After two years as Governor of the Illyrian provinces (October 1809–11) he was given command of the 6th Corps of the Army of Portugal, in place of Ney (9 April 1811). He succeeded Masséna in command of that army on 7 May.

Skilful manœuvres against Wellington ended with Marmont's over-extending his army near Salamanca (22 July 1812). Wellington was quick to seize his opportunity and go over to the offensive. Early in the battle in which the Army of Portugal was routed, Marmont was gravely wounded by a shell, which shattered one of his arms. He was compelled to give up his command, but recovered in time to command the 6th Corps of the Grand Army at Lützen, Bautzen, Dresden, Leipzig and Hanau (1813).

In the early stages of the campaign of France he fought with some success at Brienne, La Rothière, Champaubert, and Vauchamps. He won the action at Montmirail (17 February); defended Meaux (27 February); won another action at Gué à Tresmes (28 February); and took part in the capture of Reims (5 March). Thereafter things did not go so well. He was routed at Laon during the night of 9/10 March, defeated at La Fère-Champenoise (25 March) and La Ferté-Gaucher (27 March).

Marmont, Moncey and Mortier gave battle before Paris, and after putting up a good resistance opened negotiations with the Allies. Talleyrand appeared bringing overtures from the Bourbons. In his vanity Marmont felt 'that the destinies of France, of Napoleon, of all Europe, perhaps, were in his hands alone'.[1]

The Allies entered Paris next day, and a few days later (5 April), whilst negotiations were still in progress, Marmont betrayed his corps, 12,000 strong, into the hands of the Allies. It was the death knell of the Empire.

On 4 June 1814 Louis XVIII made Marmont a peer of France, and when Napoleon returned from Elba he followed the King to Ghent as commander of his Household troops, receiving from him a gift of 450,000 fr.

Napoleon proscribed Marmont (12 March 1815) and struck his name from the list of Marshals (10 April). But when the Bourbons returned he was covered with honours, which he repaid by voting for the death of Marshal Ney. He was made one of the four major-generals of the Royal Guard (3 August 1815); Minister of State (30 November 1817); Governor of the 1st Military Division at Paris (29 August 1821–30 July 1830); Ambassador Extraordinary to the Coronation of Tsar Nicholas I (April 1826) and member of the *Conseil Supérieur de la Guerre* (5 January 1828).

In the Revolution of 1830 he played once more an equivocal part, and the upshot was that he left France never to return. He lived for nearly twenty-two more years travelling in Russia, Turkey, Egypt and elsewhere, dying at Venice on 3 March 1852.

He wrote his *Memoirs* in which he attempted to justify his behaviour towards Napoleon. He also wrote a book *On Modern Armies* in which there is a chapter 'On the Reputation of Generals'. Speaking of great generals, he writes: 'In modern times, I only see Gustavus Adolphus, Turenne, Condé, Luxembourg and Napoleon, until 1812, for I am justified in reckoning among the disasters for which a General is responsible the destruction of armies caused by a want of care and excessive improvidence.'

Charles Parquin, who served in Marmont's bodyguard in Spain, speaks well of him in his Memoirs, but his defects of character are all too obvious. Marmont was the last to die of all Napoleon's Marshals. It was as if Destiny was determined to punish him for 1814, by giving him plenty of time to meditate upon his own turpitude. But his vanity was probably sufficient to permit him to live his last thirty-seven years with equanimity.

The name of Marshal Marmont is inscribed on the south face of the Arc de Triomphe de l'Étoile.

# 23

# LOUIS-GABRIEL SUCHET, DUC D'ALBUFERA

## 1770–1826

Had I two Suchets I could have held Spain for ever.

NAPOLEON

Suchet was born at Lyons on 2 March 1770, the son of a silk manu-facturer. Although he was one of the last to receive the baton he was a general of great ability, the superior in military skill to all but Masséna, Davout, Soult and, perhaps, Macdonald. He was in addition one of the few Marshals to add to his reputation in the Peninsula.

Suchet entered the cavalry of the National Guard of Lyons in 1791, and served as a *sous-lieutenant*, before becoming a soldier in the *compagnie franche*[1] of the Ardèche (12 May 1792–20 Septem-ber 1793). He soon regained his rank of *sous-lieutenant*, then was promoted captain and served at the siege of Lyons. On 20 September he was elected lieutenant-colonel of the 4th Battalion of *Voluntaires de l'Ardèche*. He took part in the siege of Toulon and in December 1793 had the distinction of capturing the wounded British General Charles O'Hara (1740?–1802).

Suchet served with the Army of Italy, and was in General Laharpe's division at the combat of Loano (23–4 November 1795). He was at Dego, Lodi and Castiglione, and was wounded by a musket shot at Cerea (12 September 1796). This did not, however, put him out of action for he served in Masséna's division at San Giorgio three days later. Arcola and Rivoli followed and he was wounded again at Neumarkt (2 April 1797). At the end of this rigorous campaign he was made provisional *chef de brigade* of the

18th of the Line. He was for a short time Chief of Staff to Brune in Switzerland (February–March 1798), and was selected to present to the Directory the colours taken at Fribourg, Neueneck and Gümenen (18 March 1798). Promoted General of Brigade (23 March), he was one of those nominated for the Army of Egypt, but did not go as he was called to Paris to defend himself from charges against his conduct in Switzerland. During 1798 and 1799 he had useful experience as Chief of Staff successively of the Armies of Italy, Mayence and the Danube.

Early in 1799 Suchet married Honorine Anthoine, daughter of the Mayor of Marseille and Marie-Anne-Rose Marseille-Clary, the sister-in-law of Joseph Bonaparte. She used often to accompany him on his campaigns.

Promoted General of Division he became Chief of Staff to the Army of Italy (10 July 1799) and served at Novi, where his gallant commander, General Barthélemy-Catherine Joubert (1769–99) was struck in the heart with a musket-ball, with the words 'Soldats! Marchez à l'ennemi!' on his lips (15 August).

On 8 January 1800 Suchet was given command of the left wing of the Army of Italy under Masséna, but got cut off from him (8 April), failed in an attack on Monte San Giacomo (19 April) and was repulsed from Loano (1 May). Retreating to the River Var he successfully held a bridgehead there (22 and 26 May). It fell to him to reoccupy Genoa (22 June) after the battle of Marengo. During the rest of the year he commanded a corps of two divisions, first under Masséna then under Brune, seeing some fighting in December, and being made Governor of Padua (21 January 1801).

On 24 July 1801 Suchet was made Inspector-General of Infantry.

In the 1805 campaign Suchet commanded a division at first under Soult, then under Lannes, serving at Ulm, Hollabrunn and Austerlitz, and being awarded the Grand Eagle of the Legion of Honour (8 February 1806).

In the 1806–7 campaign Suchet fought at Saalfeld, Jena, Pultusk, and Ostrolenka (16 February 1807). On 24 February he was given the 1st Division of Masséna's (5th) Corps, which he took over, provisionally, in August 1807.

SUCHET
*From the painting by Jean-Baptiste-Paulin Guérin, engraved by R. A. Muller.*

Honours now came thick and fast: chevalier of the *Couronne de Fer*; commander of the Order of Saint Henry of Saxony, and Count of the Empire (19 March 1808).

From 1808 to 1814 he served continuously in Spain, first as a divisional then as a corps commander, mostly in Catalonia. He was on the whole remarkably successful, proving himself a business-like administrator. After covering the siege of Saragossa, he was given command of the Army of Aragon, with which he defeated the army of General Joachim Blake (d. 1827) at Maria (15 June), and Belchite (18 June). He failed before Valencia in March 1810, but after taking Lerida, Mequinenza and Tortosa, laid siege to Tarragona, the capture of which (28 June 1811) won him his baton (8 July).

The Marshal defeated Blake once more at La Puebla de Benequasil (1 October), and won the battle of Sagunto, where he was wounded in the shoulder by a musket ball (25 October). He then blockaded and besieged Valencia which capitulated on 10 January 1812.

On 24 January Suchet was created Duke of Albufera, the only Marshal to whom Napoleon awarded a Spanish title.

Suchet's run of success was broken at Castalla on 13 April 1813 where he was defeated by Lt-General Sir John Murray (1768?–1827), who laid siege to Tarragona, but Suchet succeeded in relieving the place on 12 June, and again on 15 August.

On 15 November 1813 the Marshal was made Governor of Catalonia, and on the 18th took Bessières's place as Colonel-General of the Imperial Guard.

Suchet won the battle of Molins del Rey (15 January 1814), but events elsewhere in the Peninsula compelled him to evacuate Catalonia in April. He withdrew his army in excellent order. He now became Commander-in-Chief of the Army of the South (22 April).

After the first abdication he continued to serve, and the Bourbons made him a peer of France (4 June) and a commander of Saint-Louis (24 September). In 1815 Napoleon gave him command of the Army of the Alps (26 April), with which he made a brief invasion of Savoy (14–30 June). On 12 July he concluded an armistice with the Austrians by which he evacuated his native city of Lyons. It seems strange that the Emperor should have allotted such a minor role in this campaign to a commander of Suchet's ability. One is inclined to agree with Chandler[2] that 'Marshal Suchet would have made a far better chief of staff than Soult'. And had Soult, not Ney, commanded the left wing of the Army of the North the story of Quatre Bras and Waterloo might have been very different.

At the Second Restoration Suchet's name was struck from the list of peers of France and he was deprived of his command, but he was made a peer once more on 5 March 1819. In his last years the Marshal played but little part in public affairs, dying at the Château de Saint-Joseph or Montredon near Marseille on 3 January 1826.

Few indeed of the twenty-six could equal Suchet's record, whether for military ability or personal integrity.

# 24

# LAURENT, COMTE PUIS MARQUIS DE GOUVION-SAINT-CYR

## 1764–1830

> The Owl.
> *Nickname of Marshal Gouvion-Saint-Cyr*

..................................................................................

Gouvion-Saint-Cyr was born at Toul (Meurthe-et-Moselle) and was an artist, a painter. He was living in Paris at the outbreak of the Revolution, and enrolled as a volunteer in the 1st Battalion of the *Chasseurs Républicains*, but not until 1 September 1792, when the Revolution had been running its course for three years. His promotion was rapid. He was already a sergeant-major at the end of his first month's service, and a captain exactly two months after he joined the army! He served with the Army of the Rhine from 1792 to 1797, holding a number of staff appointments. When he had been in the army about fourteen months he was already chief of staff of a division (November 1793) and a month later he was commanding a brigade, with which he distinguished himself at Bertsheim (2–9 December 1793). He seems to have won favour in the eyes of the Representative of the People, Hentz, for he nominated Gouvion-Saint-Cyr provisional General of Brigade on 5 June 1794, and provisional General of Division five days later. The Committee of Public Safety confirmed him in the latter rank on 2 September 1794.

Gouvion-Saint-Cyr played an important part in the blockade and siege of Mayence. He stormed the *Redoute de Merlin* (1 December 1795) and evidently earned Kléber's confidence, for the latter gave him command of four divisions of the Army of the

GOUVION–SAINT–CYR
*From the painting by Horace Vernet.*

# EMMANUEL, MARQUIS DE GROUCHY

..............................................................................

Aide-de-camp de Berthier (left)

..............................................................................

(right) Officier d'Ordonnance de Murat, 1812

Rhine detached to blockade Mayence (9 October 1795). There was a great deal of fighting on the Rhine front and Gouvion-Saint-Cyr missed little of it. At the battle of Ettlingen in particular (9 July 1796) he played a decisive part. For a few weeks (10 September–6 October 1797) he commanded the Army of the Rhin-et-Moselle, being nominated by General Louis-Lazare Hoche (1768–97) when he was on his death-bed.

Though selected for the Army of England (12 January 1798), Gouvion-Saint-Cyr was sent to command at Rome, in place of Masséna (26 March). There he served under Brune. He was dismissed for abusing his powers (25 July), but was soon re-employed again as a divisional commander with the *Armée de Mayence* (16 August). Posted to the Army of the Danube he fought at Stockach (25 March 1799) and later the same year with the Army of Italy at Novi (15 August). Appointed Governor of Genoa (September), he gained some minor successes in that area, for one of which, Albaro (15 December) he received a sabre of honour. From 17 December 1799 to 6 June 1800 he was with the Army of the Rhine, serving during most of that time as second-in-command to General Jean-Victor Moreau (1763–1813), and winning the action at Biberach on 9 May 1800.

Gouvion-Saint-Cyr was made a Councillor of State (*section de la guerre*) on 22 September 1800. He was next given the task of directing the Franco-Spanish offensive against Portugal (4 February 1801). He was then sent as Ambassador to Spain (2 November). On 14 May 1803 he was made lieutenant-general commanding the Corps of Observation in the Kingdom of Naples, and he served in Italy in the 1805 campaign, capturing the Prince de Rohan and all his corps at Castelfranco (28 November) before returning to the Army of Naples.

Although Napoleon did not include Gouvion-Saint-Cyr among his first eighteen marshals, he made him Colonel-General of Cuirassiers (6 July 1804), awarded him the Grand Eagle of the Legion of Honour (2 February 1805), and created him a Count of the Empire (May 1808).

Gouvion-Saint-Cyr was made commander-in-chief of the 1st

Reserve Corps (Camp de Boulogne) on 15 December 1806. His next active service was in Spain where he commanded in Catalonia for about a year. He met with some success, taking Rosas (5 December 1808), relieving Barcelona (17 December) and winning the battles of Molins del Rey (21 December) and Valls (25 February 1809). He then laid siege to Gerona, but laid down his command before the arrival of his successor for which he was rightly disgraced. He remained unemployed until 1812, when he was selected to command the Bavarian Corps of the Grand Army (8 February). He served under Oudinot at Polotsk (17 August) and according to Marbot was far from co-operative. But Oudinot was wounded and handed over the command to Gouvion-Saint-Cyr, who completed General Wittgenstein's discomfiture, though wounded himself (18 August). For this victory he was promoted Marshal. He was wounded again more seriously at the second battle of Polotsk, where he received a musket ball in the foot, and was defeated. He then gave up his command. But by January 1813 he was sufficiently recovered to act as military adviser to Prince Eugène who had succeeded Murat in command of the Grand Army on the 24th.

On 16 February Gouvion-Saint-Cyr assumed command of the 11th Corps of the Grand Army in Augereau's stead, but fell sick and was relieved by Macdonald on 10 March. At the head of the 14th Corps he defended Dresden (25 August), and commanded the French centre in the battle of Dresden (26–7 August). He was then put in charge of the defence of that city (September), where he capitulated (11 November), and was taken prisoner.

The Marshal returned home in June 1814, and was made a peer of France on the 4th. Given command of the army formed at Orleans to resist Napoleon (19 March 1815), he was abandoned by his troops, and took refuge at Bourges (24 March). He kept aloof during the Hundred Days, but after Waterloo was a member of the Council of Defence at Paris, though he advised resistance in vain. From 8 July to 25 September 1815 he was Minister of War, succeeding Davout. At the trial of Marshal Ney he voted not for death but for deportation. Strangely enough he was an efficient Minister of Marine from 23 June to 12 September 1817. In that year he was made a Marquis and given the Grand Cross of Saint-Louis. He was Minister of War for a second time from 12 September 1817 to 18 November 1819, retiring thereafter to the country where he occupied himself with agriculture and writing his Memoirs.

Gouvion-Saint-Cyr was known in the army as *l'hibou*, the Owl. According to Marbot, who served with him in 1812, he was something of a recluse, and preferred to shut himself up and play the violin, rather than engage in the more mundane tasks of a general, such as visiting his wounded. Macdonald thought him a talented man and a clever soldier. If his advancement was slow compared to that of rough old grenadiers like Lefebvre and Oudinot, it was because the Emperor did not feel that he could depend upon his devotion.

# PRINCE JOSEF ANTON PONIATOWSKI
## 1763–1813

Il faut mourir en brave.
PONIATOWSKI AT LEIPZIG
*19 October 1813*

Prince Josef Poniatowski was born on 7 May 1763, not at Warsaw, as is frequently stated,[1] but at the Kinsky Palace in the Herrengasse in Vienna. His father was Andrew Poniatowski, a general in the Austrian service, and his mother was Theresa Kinsky. But though born in an Austrian palace, *ein Wiener Kind,* having Lithuanian, Czech and Italian blood in his veins and dying in the German River Elster, he was nevertheless Polish through and through.

Poniatowski joined the Austrian Army in February 1780 and in consequence of the wishes of the Empress Maria Theresa, he was commissioned straight away as a cornet in the 2nd Regiment of Carabiniers, whose honorary colonel was the Grand-Duke Francis, later the Emperor Francis II. In old Marshal Lacy, the titular colonel, Poniatowski found both a patron and a mentor.

In September 1781 the young prince, who was diligent as well as having influence, became second-in-command of a squadron; in January 1782 he became a squadron commander and in September 1784 was promoted major. He fought a duel with a comrade who had cast some slur on the memory of his father. Soon after, during the summer manœuvres he swam his horse, fully accoutred, across the Elbe which was in flood after torrential rain. A Bohemian soothsayer drew his horoscope, and she spoke the prophetic words:

*Der Elbe Herr bist du gewarden,*
*doch eine Elster wird dich morden.*

In January 1785 he became the second lieutenant-colonel of the light horse regiment of Levenehr, and in 1786 the senior lieutenant-colonel. In the autumn of that year he was transferred to the Emperor Joseph II's Light Horse, a *corps d'élite*, in which a Captain Mack was serving: this was 'the unfortunate Mack' who was to surrender Ulm to Napoleon in 1805.

Poniatowski made a visit to Berlin and was presented to King Frederick William II (1786–97), who bestowed upon him the Orders of Saint Stanislas and of the White Eagle. He also paid a visit to the Court of the Empress Catherine II of Russia.

In January 1788 the Prince was made A.D.C. to the Emperor Joseph II, with whom he made his first campaign. But before he set out, he attended the first night of Mozart's *Don Giovanni*. Among the companions of his first campaign against the Turks was another young prince, Karl von Schwarzenberg, who was to command the Austrian Army against Napoleon.

Leading a column against the citadel of Sabatch on the River Sava (24 April 1788) he got across the ditch with some 15 men, only to be hit in the thigh with grape at point-blank range. He was saved by the devotion of a Croatian soldier, one Kerner, who was to remain in his service for the rest of his days. His doctor, surprisingly enough in those days of primitive surgery, managed to prevent his being lamed for life.

In November 1788 the Emperor made him supernumerary second colonel of his light horse regiment, in recognition of his services to the House of Austria and in the hope that in the future they would not be lacking. This was the reward of the experience he had acquired, his praiseworthy courage and other good qualities. Hardly had he recovered from his wounds when the Prince asked to be sent on his second Turkish campaign. He was colonel designate of the Regiment of Modena when the Grand Diet of Warsaw called upon him to serve his own country. He retired therefore from the Austrian service and by August 1789 he was in Warsaw. In the spring of 1790 he was given command of a division in the Ukraine, where in 1792 he had to make head against three times his numbers. He had the modesty to ask King Stanislas II, who was his uncle,

PONIATOWSKI
*Engraved by Charles State.*

to confide the command to a more knowing commander: 'We can
fight, but we cannot make war', he said when he left for the front.
His men were inexperienced, ill-equipped and poorly trained.

On 18 June he fought General Markov at Zielence, and – rather unexpectedly – repulsed the Russians with loss. With his habitual candour he attributed this to chance! In fact he never forgave himself for not making the most of the opportunities he had won. But, having been brought up in the methodical school of the Austrian Army, to whom the novel *blitzkreig* Italian campaign of 1796 would scarcely have been credible, this was like being wise *before* the event. In this affair he led the Potocki battalion under fire, exposing his person as always, but, as was his way, mentioning nothing of his own dangers in his dispatches. When his uncle, and king, heard in a roundabout way of his exploits, he wrote to him: 'Remember that you are the soul of the army, which will become a corpse, and which, if she loses you, will remain but a corpse.' But unhappily the pusillanimous man who paid him this just tribute lacked the fundamental courage to stand up to the Russian invasion. After disagreements with the Diet the Prince left Poland after the Treaty of Targowica, and joined the Polish volunteers under General Kościuszko, who gave him command of a division in 1794. In 1795 he refused to serve as a Russian general and retired to Vienna and then to his estates near Warsaw (1798). In 1806 the King of Prussia nominated him Governor of Warsaw, and on 18 December he was made Minister of War in the provisional government with the rank of General of Division. On 2 January 1807 he became the commander of the 1st Polish Legion in the French service.

Under the Empire honours, awards and distinctions came his way in full measure.

4 June 1807: Pension of 29,500 fr.

1808: Minister of War of the Grand Duchy of Warsaw with the rank of Generalissimo.

1809: Grand Eagle of the Legion of Honour.

Grand Cordon of the Military Order of the Grand Duchy of Warsaw.

Gift of a million francs from the King of Saxony.

In the 1809 campaign he fought the Archduke Ferdinand at Fallenti (19 April), retreated on Warsaw, then counterattacked and took Lublin and other places before occupying Cracow in

July. After the peace he founded schools of artillery and engineering and a military hospital in Warsaw.

In 1812 Poniatowski commanded the 5th Corps (Polish) of the Grand Army (3 March 1812), which he led at Smolensk and Borodino.

The Prince was wounded at the Berezina (26 November 1812), but was sufficiently recovered to reorganize the Polish Army in December. He commanded the 8th Corps (Polish) (12 March 1813) in Poland, and, rejoining the Grand Army in July, invaded Bohemia and won actions at Lobau (9 September), Altenburg (2 October), Chemnitz (4 October) – though he was driven from the place the same day – and Penig (8 October), which he evacuated next day. He was wounded by a lance thrust in an affair on the Rotha road (9 October) but commanded the right of Napoleon's Army at Leipzig (16–18 October).

The Emperor made Poniatowski a Marshal on 16 October. On the 19th he got cut off from the Grand Army and charged a mass of enemy skirmishers at the head of a handful of cavalry. Wounded four times and fainting from loss of blood, he plunged on horseback into the River Elster and was drowned. The last words that his staff heard from his lips were 'Poland' and 'Honour'. There is a good life, *Le Prince Joseph Poniatowski* by Szymon Askenazy.

Poniatowski was above all a cavalryman – *le Bayard polonais*. Military theory was not, perhaps, his strong point. But among the Polish commanders of his day he was eclipsed only by General Jan Henryk Dombrowski (1755–1818), his successor in command of the 8th Corps. For this assertion we have the authority not only of the Emperor himself but of that stern warrior, Marshal Davout. Under fire the best commanders are not *always* the best Staff College students.

The name of Marshal Poniatowski is inscribed on the east side of the Arc de Triomphe de l'Étoile.

# EMMANUEL, MARQUIS DE GROUCHY
## 1766–1847

Soixante batailles, plus de cent combats, où la victoire fut dans presque tous arrosée du sang de ce général, sont des titres glorieux qui le feront admirer des guerriers de tous les temps.

FASTES. II. 65

None of the twenty-six Marshals of the Empire has been more roughly handled by posterity than the last to receive his baton. It may be argued that Grouchy made mistakes during the 1815 campaign: the same may be said of the Emperor himself. But it cannot be denied that Grouchy was a brave soldier and a man of honour.

Grouchy was born of a noble family in Paris on 23 October 1766, became a cadet at the Strasbourg Artillery School on 31 March 1780 – at the ripe old age of 13! – being commissioned lieutenant on 14 March 1781, with effect from 23 October 1780. He was posted to the Besançon Regiment of Artillery (24 August 1781), but in 1784 transferred to the cavalry, becoming a captain in *Royal-Étranger* (28 October) and two years later a *sous-lieutenant* (ranking, however, as a lieutenant-colonel!) in the Scots Company of the Royal *Gardes du Corps* (25 December 1786).

Grouchy was in favour of the Revolution, which did not enjoy the support of many senior officers of the cavalry. In consequence his advancement was rapid, if not smooth.

18 December 1791: Lt-Colonel, 12th Chasseurs à Cheval.
 1 February 1792: Colonel, 2nd Dragoons.
 8 July 1792: Colonel, 6th Hussars.
 7 September 1792: Maréchal de Camp.

GROUCHY
*From the painting by Jean-Sébastien Rouillard, engraved by Henry Wolf.*

23 April 1795:      General of Division (provisional).

During the Revolutionary Wars Grouchy had a career full of variety. He repulsed an attack by Charette and his Vendéens on Nantes (31 August–1 September 1793), and was wounded soon after (5 September). He was then suspended from his employment by the Decree of the Convention which excluded all nobles from any military employment. His soldiers surrounded his Head-quarters hoping to be allowed to keep him as their chief, but he slipped away. Soon afterwards the Vendéens crossed the River Loire, and to resist them Grouchy assembled the National Guard of the canton to which he had retired, marching with them as a private soldier and asking, with remarkably good taste, 'If I am not permitted to lead our columns against the enemy, what unjust power can forbid my shedding my blood for the cause of the People?'

Reinstated on the fall of Robespierre, he was Chief of Staff to Hoche when he defeated the *émigré* French troops who had landed in Quiberon Bay (1795). When at length the Vendéens were crushed, Grouchy went with Hoche on the abortive Bantry Bay Expedition (24 December 1796–18 January 1797). He next smelt powder in Italy, where he was victorious in a bloody affair at San Giuliano (20 June 1799), when two of his A.D.C.s were killed by his side, and two others badly wounded. He commanded a division at Novi, where, in defending the village of Pasturana, he received no less than fourteen wounds before he and his A.D.C., Captain Chevalier, fell into the hands of the Austrians. He insisted that the latter's wounds should be attended to before his own. He was released after Marengo, in time to fight at Hohenlinden, where he contributed greatly to the victory of his friend Moreau. When, not long after, the latter was disgraced, Grouchy could not bring himself to believe that he was a traitor. None the less Napoleon continued to employ him.

Grouchy commanded the 2nd Division of Marmont's (2nd) Corps in the Grand Army (30 August 1805) and was at Ulm. In the Prussian campaign of 1806 he commanded the 2nd Division of Dragoons belonging to Murat's Reserve Cavalry (20 September

1806). At Zehdenick (26 October) he cut up the Queen of Prussia's Dragoon Regiment. At Prenzlow (28 October) by an audacious charge at the head of his dragoons he compelled Prince Hohenlohe's troops to surrender. Wounded at Eylau, he recovered in time to distinguish himself at Friedland. He was rewarded with the Grand Cross of the Military Order of Bavaria (29 June 1807) and the Grand Eagle of the Legion of Honour (13 July). He was also a Commander of the *Couronne de Fer*.

Grouchy was commanding the cavalry of the Army of Spain when on 2 May 1808 the revolt (known as the *Dos de Mayo*) broke out in Madrid. Grouchy repressed it, but not before he had had a horse killed under him. Sent to Italy, he served with great success, commanding the 1st Dragoon Division under the Viceroy, Eugène de Beauharnais, in the 1809 campaign. After a series of victories in the plains of Udine and on the banks of the River Isonzo, he joined up with the Grand Army in time for the battle of Wagram. He now succeeded Marmont (31 July 1809) as Colonel-General of Chasseurs.

In 1812 Grouchy took command of the 3rd Corps of the Reserve Cavalry (28 January). He was wounded in the chest by a grapeshot at Borodino, but recovered in time to command the famous *bataillon sacré*, composed entirely of officers, which guarded the Emperor during the retreat (November).

Owing to ill-health Grouchy played no part in the 1813 campaign but as commander-in-chief of the cavalry of the Grand Army, as it was still called, he played a courageous and active part in the Campaign of France of 1814. He fought at Brienne, La Rothière, Vauchamps, Montmirail, at the capture of Troyes (23 February) where he was wounded, at Braisne (5 March) and Craonne, where he was shot in the thigh. Under the Bourbons he was employed as inspector-general of chasseurs and lancers (19 July 1814), but the following year he commanded the *Armée du Midi* and captured the Duc d'Angoulême.

Napoleon made Grouchy a Marshal on 15 April 1815 and a Peer of France on 2 June, and it would be difficult to deny his claim to these honours. He then gave him command of the right

'The Abdication, Fontainebleau, April 6, 1814', from the painting by Étienne Prosper Berne-Bellecour. Napoleon is dressed in his favourite uniform as a Colonel of the Chasseurs of the Guard. The group of four Marshals are, from left to right, Ney, Lefebvre, Oudinot, Macdonald. On the right stands Flahaut.

wing of the Army of the North, a charge for which his previous experience as a corps commander of cavalry was not necessarily the best preparation. Charged with the pursuit of the Prussians after Ligny, he was held up at Wavre. General Gérard, one of his corps commanders and himself a future Marshal, urged Grouchy to 'march to the sound of the guns', but even had he done so, it is doubtful whether he could have reached the field of Waterloo in time to influence the fate of the day. At the crisis of the battle Napoleon, hoping to encourage his men to a last effort, sent a colonel along his line crying 'Voilà Grouchy!' When the Prussians appeared instead, the French blamed not Napoleon but Grouchy – and have been doing so ever since. In fact on hearing the news of Waterloo Grouchy effected the withdrawal of his wing in the most handsome fashion, and had the Emperor been in the mood to fight on he might have used this corps as the nucleus of a new army.

Grouchy was proscribed at the Second Restoration, and his name was struck from the list of marshals (1 August). He escaped to America. In 1819 as the result of an amnesty he was given the rank of lieutenant-general, returning to France next year, and retiring from the army in 1824. He was recognized once more as a Marshal of France (19 November 1831), and as a Peer of France on 11 October 1832. He died at Saint-Étienne on 29 May 1847.

# Notes on the Text

ANNALS OF THE MARSHALS
1. He had previously been in the Dutch service.
2. He was already Duke of Ragusa (1808).


THE CAREERS OF THE MARSHALS
Chapter 2
1. (1774–1833). Later Duke of Rovigo (1808).
2. Now La Bastide-Murat.
3. Later the Chasseurs à Cheval de Champagne, then the 12th Chasseurs.
4. General Pierre Dupont de l'Éstang (1765–1840), who capitulated to General Castaños at Bailén on 22 July 1808.
5. Many of them were on Prussian chargers taken in the Jena campaign.
6. Major-General Sir Hudson Lowe, K.B. (1769–1844) was to be Governor of St Helena during Napoleon's captivity there (1815–21). He was promoted lieutenant-general in 1830.
7. Eugène de Beauharnais.
8. Scene of a British commando landing in 1943.


Chapter 3
1. A very free translation would be 'If only everyone had been as upright as me'.


Chapter 4
1. Guillotined in Paris, 16 November 1793.


Chapter 5
1. In the words of a contemporary: 'Berthier est fait prince de Wagram. La dignité eût mieux convenu à Masséna, premier héros de cette rude journée.'
2. Jac Weller. *Wellington in the Peninsula, 1808–1814*, p. 135 (London, 1962).


Chapter 7
1. David G. Chandler. *The Campaigns of Napoleon*, p. 497 (London/New York, 1966).
2. 'Free-and-easy'.


Chapter 8
1. Henri de La Tour d'Auvergne, Vicomte de Turenne (1611–75). Marshal, 16 May 1643; Marshal-General, 5 April 1660.
2. Louis-Claude Hector, Duc de Villars (1652–1734). Marshal, 20 October 1702; Marshal-General, 18 October 1733.
3. Arminius-Maurice, Comte de Saxe (1696–1750). Marshal, 26 March 1744; Marshal-General, 12 January 1747.
4. According to Lieutenant James Hope (92nd Highlanders) Soult was court-martialled and punished during the time he was a Corporal. Hope stayed in

1815 at the Château de Rique near Montreuil and his host had been Soult's captain under the Old Régime. See *A British Officer. Letters from Portugal, Spain, and France during the Memorable Campaigns of 1811, 1812 and 1813; and from Belgium and France in the year 1815* (Edinburgh, 1819).

5. 'It is impossible by any description to do justice to the distinguished gallantry of the troops; but every individual nobly did his duty; and it is observed that our dead, particularly the 57th Regiment, were lying as they fought, in ranks, and every wound was in the front' (Beresford).

6. Jac Weller. *Wellington in the Peninsula, 1808–1814*, p. 185 (London, 1962).

7. *Ibid*, pp. 275–6.

8. His wife was Jeanne-Louise-Élisabeth Berg. She survived him by only three months. It is said that she had often accompanied him on his campaigns.

## Chapter 10

1. General Anne-Jean-Marie-René Savary, Duc de Rovigo (1774–1833). He took over the 5th Corps from Lannes when the latter fell ill (31 January 1807).

## Chapter 12

1. Which became in 1791 the 5th Hussars.

2. 'Warrant officer, Class I' might not be too bad a translation of something that is not really translatable.

3. Baron Jomini rose to be a general in the Russian service.

4. *Treatise on Grand Military Operations*, 8 vols. (Paris, 1811–16).

5. Jac Weller. *Wellington in the Peninsula, 1808–1814*, p. 134 (London, 1962).

6. According to Chandler (see *The Campaigns of Napoleon*, p. 801) he was wounded four times, but neither Martinien (*Tableaux par corps et par batailles des officiers tués et blessés . . . 1805–1815*) nor Six (*Dictionnaire biographique des généraux . . .*) mentions him being hit on this occasion.

7. Borodino.

## Chapter 13

1. *In Napoleonic Days*.

2. In 1787 Monsieur Davout, chevalier of Saint-Louis, was Major of XV Royal-Champagne, at Hesdin. Davout *fil*, appears in the list as *Sous-Lieutenan* (sic) *de remplacement*, so it seems that he took rank in his corps whilst still at the Military School. (M. de Roussel. *État Militaire de France Pour l' Année 1787*, pp. 375, 376 [Paris, 1887]. Author's collection.)

3. Pichegru was imprisoned in the Temple for his part in Georges Cadoudal's conspiracy, and was found strangled in his cell on 5 April 1804.

## Chapter 15

1. Kellermann was one of the peers who voted for the death penalty at the trial of Marshal Ney.

## Chapter 18

1. He was not a count under the Old Régime, but was made one by Napoleon in 1808.

Chapter 19
1. 'Beau-Soleil' might be translated 'Handsome Sun', or 'Sun in Splendour', whilst 'Bellune' (Belle-Lune) = 'Beautiful Moon'.

Chapter 20
1. 'It is on the field of battle that has done you honour, where I owe you the great part of yesterday's success, that I make you Marshal of France; you have long deserved it.'
2. Marshal of France, 3 July 1816, and Marquis, 1817.

Chapter 21
1. R. F. Delderfield, in *The March of the Twenty-Six: the Story of Napoleon's Marshals* (p. 27) makes it 34! Georges Six in *Dictionnaire biographique des généraux* . . . (pp. 275–7) mentions 22 specific wounds.

Chapter 22
1. William Milligan Sloane. *The Life of Napoleon Bonaparte*, vol. iv, p. 133 (New York/London, 1896).

Chapter 23
1. Independent company.
2. p. 1022.

Chapter 25
1. Even the admirable Georges Six fell into this error.

# Notes on the Colour Plates

*Berthier and Guide.* The Marshal is in full dress, though without the Grand Cordon of the Legion of Honour. It was in this uniform that he rode beside the Emperor on campaign. The mameluke sabre was popular at the period, not only among officers who had served in Egypt. The Guide is a senior N.C.O., and wears the handsome, if plain, walking-out dress for summer, about the year 1808. The uniform was not unlike that of the dragoons of the period. (cf. *Les Uniformes du l<sup>er</sup> Empire*, 117 Series, Vol. I, Chap. VI, drawing by E. Bucquoy, 1916.)

*Murat and 1809 Offiicier d'Ordonnance.* Murat is shown here as King of Naples in one of the uniforms which he devised for himself. His talent for sartorial design was unlimited. Murat had about ten *officiers d'Ordonnance*, young Frenchmen and Neapolitans, to transmit his orders in the field. The most distinctive features of this uniform were the shako and pelisse.

*Moncey and Éclaireur-Guide.* The Marshal is shown in full ceremonial uniform wearing his cloak (*manteau de cour*). Portraits exist showing other Marshals in this attire, but it would seem they did not all go to the same tailor. In some cases the cut of the coat conceals the embroidered waistcoat. Most of the Marshals wore lace cuffs, but very few had the white garter knots with gold fringes.

The *manteau* is of blue velvet, lined with silk, and suspended from a cord rather in the fashion of a hussar's pelisse.

The hat (*chapeau de cérémonie*) is ornamented with ostrich plumes.

The Marshal wears the cordon and plaque of the Grand-Eagle of the Legion of Honour, bestowed on him on 2 February 1805.

This was the costume in which the Marshals appeared at the Coronation and other great ceremonies of the Empire.

Moncey's guides, his escort during the period when he distinguished himself by his brave and skilful defence of the Barrière de Clichy, wore a uniform not unlike the *compagnie d'élite* of a regiment of *Chasseurs à cheval*. The source for this N.C.O.'s uniform is H. Boisselier's drawing for the famous series *Les Uniformes du l<sup>er</sup> Empire* published by the late Commandant Bucquoy (118 Series, Vol. I, Chap. VI, No. 1).

*Masséna.* Masséna is shown in the full dress of a Marshal who is also commander-in-chief of an army. His wily countenance has been drawn after an *aquarelle* executed on 20 October 1809 by Carl Agricola, which appears in Les Maréchaux de France by Jean Brunon.

*Bernadotte.* Bernadotte is shown in *Tenue de cérémonie*, though without the *manteau de cour* or cloak, which Augereau wears in the portrait by Robert Lefevre in the Musée de Versailles.

*Aide-de-Camp and Guide of Bernadotte.* The aide-de-camp's handsome hussar

uniform is based on a plate in *Les Tenues de Troupes de France* by Job. Bernadotte's A.D.Cs. like his guides seem to have worn uniforms of his own devising.

The duty of the guides was to escort baggage containing secret papers,
and the despatch of urgent orders. In 1805 Bernadotte succeeded Mortier as
Governor of Hanover. His guides wore a special hussar-style uniform, as his
predecessor's had done. This figure is taken from Planche 63 of the excellent
*Le Plumet* series published by Rigo. Commandant Bucquoy dedicated several
series of *Les Uniformes du 1er Empire* to *Les Guides d'Etat-Major*.

*Lannes*. The embroidery on the collar and cuffs of this undress uniform is of oak
leaf pattern. The mameluke sword lacks a sword-knot. For some reason the
Marshal is shown without either sash or sword-belt, but otherwise he is dressed
as he would have been on campaign. He wears the plaque of the Grand Eagle of
the Legion of Honour. Lannes' portrait wearing this uniform is in the Palace of
Versailles. In 1910 Bucquoy drew it for *Les Uniformes de 1er Empire* (Series 31,
No. 6).

Lannes's velvet ceremonial coat, and another worn when he was in petite
uniforme, are preserved in the Musée de l'Armée. They are illustrated in Lucien
Rousselot's plate *Maréchaux d'Empire* (*Armée Francaise*, Planche No. 100,
published in 1967).

His saddles and holsters were on view at the *Exposition Rétrospective Militaire*
in 1900. They were not regulation, the saddle being described by Rousselot as
'anglo-hussardée', from which it would seem that the Marshal used a saddle of
the sort then issued to English hussars and light dragoons.

*Suchet*. Undress uniform as worn on horseback. No doubt Suchet dressed in
this style during his campaigns in Catalonia. The most unusual feature is
the blue breeches; for the most part the Marshals seem to have worn buff
breeches when in the saddle. Compare the portrait of Suchet by Guérin (p. 171),
where the Marshal is reviewing his army on a ceremonial occasion during the
later years of the First Empire.

*Ney*. Ney is shown in the undress uniform worn when mounted. His features
are taken from a painting by Louis David (Collection Raoul et Jean Brunon,
Château de l'Emperi) which is the colour frontispiece of Jean Brunon's *Les
Maréchaux de France à travers neuf siècles d'histoire*. Ney is often called *Le
Rougeaud*, but it seems that his hair, if fair, was not exactly red.

*Mortier and Guide*. The Marshal is shown in his uniform as *colonel-général
de l'Artillerie et des Matelots de la Garde*, which was, of course, a uniform
peculiar to himself. It was a uniform for special ceremonial occasions. He is
shown in his full dress (mounted) in his portrait by Ponce-Camus (p. 99).
Bucquoy (12th Series, No. 8) represents Mortier in his colonel-general's uniform
mounted on a bay horse with gold trappings, and a leopard skin shabracque
edged with gold and mounted on red cloth. As a colonel-general Mortier was
entitled to wear an aiguillette, but his portraits do not show one. The guides
wore a handsome hussar-style uniform. The bridle etc. were of black leather,
and the shabracque was of green cloth, edged with yellow. The plume is
sometimes shown as half black and half green, the latter being uppermost.
The guides had carbines as well as sabres, slung from buff belts. Bucquoy and

Knötel both illustrate Mortier's guides, but the most useful and easily available reference is probably *Le Plumet, Planche 64.*

*Bessières.* The Marshal wears the uniform of colonel-general of the cavalry of the Imperial Guard, which was his normal wear. The Marshal was rather old-fashioned and continued to wear a queue after the rest of the army had cut them off. It will be observed that the uniform resembles the undress of the Chasseurs of the Guard. (cf. Lucien Rousselot, *Maréchaux d'Empire*, Detail 17.) As a colonel-general Bessières wears an aiguillette.

*Davout.* The Marshal is shown in the campaign uniform that he wore at Auerstädt and elsewhere. Davout was colonel-general of the Grenadiers of the Old Guard, and that is why he wore an aiguillette. Davout was very short-sighted and wore spectacles, but we have taken his features from a painting by Berthon (*Musée de Versailles*) in which these are not shown.

An undress coat belonging to the Marshal is in the Collection Raoul et Jean Brunon. It had fallen into the hands of the Russians in Davout's personal baggage wagon during the retreat from Moscow! Monsieur Jean Brunon showed this garment to the author in 1963. It seemed rather small for a big man, and tight in the sleeves.

*Marmont.* The Marshal is shown in the uniform of colonel-general of Hussars and *Chasseurs à cheval*, a uniform, one may remark, which is rather that of the former than the latter. It appears to have no connection with any particular regiment. H. Feist drew this uniform in 1908 for Bucquoy's 12th Series. He showed Marmont on a chestnut charger with gold harness and a leopard-skin shabracque, hussar style, trimmed with gold lace and mounted on green cloth.

*Poniatowski.* This picture is based upon a contemporary coloured engraving reproduced in *The Anatomy of Glory* by Henry Lachoque and Anne S. K. Brown (Lund Humphries 1961).

*Grouchy.* The Marshal is shown in the uniform of colonel-general of Chasseurs, an appointment which he assumed in 1809, nearly six years before he became a Marshal.

*Aide-de-Camp of Berthier and 1812 Officier d'Ordonnance of Murat.* This officer appears in *tenue de société*, wearing a coat cut *à la chasseur*, which may be of scarlet because Berthier was Prince of Neuchâtel, a principality which favoured that colour for its uniforms.

In addition to this uniform the A.D.Cs. had summer and winter campaign uniforms and a parade dress which resembled those of hussars.

In 1812 Berthier had seven A.D.Cs. and two provisional (extra) A.D.Cs. They were: Colonel Baron Flahaut, Colonel Baron Lejeune, Colonel Baron Sopranzy, Chef d'Escadrons Comte de Montesquiou, Chef d'Escardrons Baron de Noailles, Chef de Bataillon Baron Bernet, Lieutenant Baron Leisulteux; and Chef d'Escardrons de Bongars and Chef d'Escardrons Baron Fezensac.

Murat's *officier d'Ordonnance* is shown here in the 1812 campaign uniform which should be compared with the earlier version above. The collar and cuffs are of the sky-blue colour traditional for French A.D.Cs.

Needless to say the Marshals and their entourage had a variety of other uniforms besides those shown here. Readers who wish to pursue the subject further are recommended to obtain Rousselot's plates and especially No. 100, and the *Le Plumet* plates, particularly Nos. 39, 40, 41, 63, 68, 74 and 85. Bucquoy's series pioneered in this field, and some of his work has been reproduced in *Tradition*. Dr. Heurtoulle's series may also be recommended with confidence.

# Appendix 1

## Napoleonic Generals who were made Marshals of France after 1815

1815
HENRI-JACQUES-GUILLAUME CLARKE (1765–1818), Comte d'Hunebourg, Duc de Feltre. General of Brigade, 1793; of Division, 1803; Governor of Berlin, 1806; Minister of War, 1807.

1823
JACQUES-ALEXANDRE-BERNARD LAW (1768–1828), Comte, *puis* Marquis de Lauriston. General of Brigade, 1802; Division, 1803. Governor of Ragusa, 1806, and Venice, 1807. Count, 1808; Marquis, 1817.

1824
GABRIEL-JEAN-JOSEPH, COMTE MOLITOR (1770–1849). General of Brigade, 1799; Division, 1800; Count, 1808.

1829
NICOLAS-JOSEPH, MARQUIS MAISON (1771–1840). General of Brigade, 1806; Division, 1812. Baron, 1808; Marquis, 1817.

1830
LOUIS-AUGUSTE-VICTOR DE BOURMONT, COMTE DE GHAISNES (1773–1846). General of Brigade, 1813; Division, 1814. Deserted Napoleon just before Waterloo. Took Algiers, 1830. He was only a Marshal for a month as he was exiled because of the Revolution of July 1830.

MAURICE-ETIENNE, COMTE GÉRARD (1773–1852). General of Brigade, 1806; Division, 1812; Baron, 1809. Commanded the 4th Corps at Ligny and Wavre, 1815. Took Antwerp, 1832.

1831
BERTRAND, COMTE CLAUZEL (1772–1842), General of Brigade, 1799; Division, 1802; Count, 1815. Commanded at Salamanca after Marmont was wounded. Commanded the Army of Africa, 1830.

GEORGES MOUTON, COMTE DE LOBAU (1770–1838), General of Brigade, 1805; A.D.C. to the Emperor, 1805; General of Division, 1807; Comte de Lobau, 1810; commanded the 6th Corps at Waterloo.

1837
SYLVAIN-CHARLES, COMTE VALÉE (1773–1846), General of Brigade, 1809; Baron, 1811; Division, 1811; Count, 1814.

1840
HORACE-FRANÇOIS-BASTIEN, COMTE SÉBASTIANI DE LA PORTA (1772–1851). Corsican. General of Brigade, 1803; Division, 1805. Ambassador to Turkey, 1802, 1806; Count, 1809.

1843

JEAN-BAPTISTE DROUET, COMTE D'ERLON (1765–1844), General of Brigade, 1799; Division, 1803; Count, 1809; commanded the 1st Corps at Waterloo.

1847

HONORÉ-CHARLES-MICHEL-JOSEPH, COMTE REILLE (1775–1860), General of Brigade, 1803; Division, 1806; Count, 1808. Commanded the 2nd Corps at Quatre Bras and Waterloo.

GUILLAUME DODE, VICOMTE DE LA BRUNERIE (1775–1851), Baron, 1808; General of Brigade, 1809; Lt.-General, 1814; Viscount, 1823.

1850

PRINCE JÉRÔME BONAPARTE (1784–1860), Napoleon's youngest brother. Rear-Admiral, 1806; Division, 1807; King of Westphalia, 1807–1814. Commanded a division at Quatre Bras and Waterloo, being wounded at both battles. Governor of Les Invalides, 1848.

1851

RÉMY-JOSEPH-ISIDORE, BARON *puis* COMTE EXELMANS (1775–1852), General of Brigade, 1807; Baron, 1808; Division, 1812; Count, 1813; commanded the 2nd Cavalry Corps at Fleurus, Ligny and Wavre.

JEAN-ISIDORE, COMTE HARISPE (1768–1855), General of Brigade, 1807; Baron, 1808; Division, 1810; Count, 1813. Wounded at Orthez and taken at Toulouse, 1814. Adhered to the Emperor in 1815.

PHILIPPE-ANTOINE, COMTE D'ORNANO (1786–1863), General of Brigade, 1811; Division, and Count, 1812; Marshal, 1861.

In addition Thomas-Robert Bugeaud de la Piconnerie (1784–1849), the conqueror of Algeria, had commanded a battalion in the Peninsula, though he had not risen to general rank. Maréchal de Camp, 1831; Lieutenant-General, 1836. Marshal, 1843. Duc d'Isly, 1844.

# Appendix 2

## The Main Battles of the Revolution and the Empire

*1792*
20 September — Valmy
6 November — Jemappes

*1793*
18 March — Neerwinden
27 August–27 December — Siege of Toulon
6–8 September — Hondschoote
15/16 October — Wattignies

*1794*
18 May — Tourcoing
26 June — Fleurus

*1795*
27 June — The *émigrés* land at Quiberon
16–20 July — *Emigrés* are destroyed
23–25 November — Loano

*1796*
12 April — Montenotte
14–15 April — Dego
21 April — Mondovi
10 May — Lodi
3 August — Lonato
5 August — Castiglione
3 September — Würzburg
8 September — Bassano
12 November — Caldiero
15–17 November — Arcola

*1797*
15 January — Rivoli
16 January — La Favorita
18 April — Preliminary Peace of Leoben
17 October — Treaty of Campoformio

*1798*
21 July — Pyramids

*1799*
25 March — Stockach
17 April — Mount Tabor
May–June — Siege of Acre
17–19 June — The Trebbia
25 July — Abukir
15 August — Novi
25/26 September — Zürich

*1800*
4 June — Genoa capitulates
14 June — Marengo
3 December — Hohenlinden

*1805*
17 October — Surrender of Ulm
2 December — Austerlitz

*1806*
14 October — Jena and Auerstädt

*1807*
8 February — Eylau
10 June — Heilsberg
14 June — Friedland

*1808*
4 December — Napoleon takes Madrid

*1809*
16 January — Coruña
21 April — Landshut
22 April — Eckmühl
21–22 May — Aspern-Essling
5/6 July — Wagram
28 July — Talavera
19 November — Ocaña

*1810*
27 September — Busaco

*1811*

| | |
|---|---|
| 5 May | Fuentes de Oñoro |
| 16 May | La Albuera |

*1812*

| | |
|---|---|
| 22 July | Salamanca |
| 17 August | Smolensk |
| 7 September | Borodino |
| 16–17 November | Krasnoe |
| 26–28 November | Berezina |

*1813*

| | |
|---|---|
| 2 May | Lützen |
| 20–21 May | Bautzen |
| 21 June | Vitoria |
| 26 July–1 August | Sorauren |
| 26–27 August | Dresden |
| 16–19 October | Leipzig |
| 30–31 October | Hanau |

*1814*

| | |
|---|---|
| 29 January | Brienne |
| 30 January | La Rothière |
| 10 February | Champaubert |
| 11 February | Montmirail |
| 12 February | Château-Thierry |
| 14 February | Vauchamps |
| 18 February | Montereau |
| 27 February | Orthez |
| 7 March | Craonne |
| 9–10 March | Laon |
| 13 March | Reims |
| 20–21 March | Arcis-sur-Aube |
| 25 March | La Fère-Champenoise |
| 30 March | Paris |
| 10 April | Toulouse |

*1815*

| | |
|---|---|
| 16 June | Ligny and Quatre Bras |
| 18 June | Waterloo and Wavre |

# Select Bibliography

Anon. Les Fastes de La Gloire or *Les Braves, recommended to Posterity ; Monument erected to the defenders of* la Patrie: *By a society of Men of Letters and Soldiers.* Paris, 1825. It is essentially a patriotic work, citing the individual feats and careers of soldiers who distinguished themselves under the Revolution, the Consulate and the Empire.

Askenazy, Szymon. *Le Prince Joseph Poniatowski* (Paris, 1921).

Brunon, Jean. *Les Maréchaux de France à travers neuf siècles d'histoire.*

Bucquoy, Eugène Louis. *Les Gardes d'honneur du premier Empire* (Nancy, 1908). *Les Uniformes de l'armée française. Terre-mer-air* (Paris, 1935).

Chandler, David G. *The Campaigns of Napoleon* (London/New York, 1966).

Cronin, Vincent. *Napoleon* (London, 1971). [A very sympathetic life of the Emperor, showing him in the most favourable light]

Delderfield, R. F. *The March of the Twenty-Six : the Story of Napoleon's Marshals* (London, 1962).

Dupuy, R. Ernest & Trevor N. *The Encyclopedia of Military History from 3500 B.C. to the Present* (London, 1970).

Fraser, Edward. *The War Drama of the Eagles: Napoleon's Standard-bearers on the Battlefield in Victory and Defeat from Austerlitz to Waterloo* (London, 1912).

Hourtoulle, I. G. *Soldats et uniformes du prémier Empire* (Paris, n.d.).

Lachouque, Henry. *The Anatomy of Glory. Napoleon and his Guard: a study in leadership.* Adapted from the French by Anne S. K. Brown (London/New York, 1961).

Larchey, Lorédan (ed.). *The Narrative of Captain Coignet, Soldier of the Empire, 1776-1850.* Translated by Mrs M. Carey (London, 1897).

Le Barrois d'Orgeval. *Le Maréchalat de France des Origines à Nos Jours.* 2 vols. (Paris, 1932).

Marbot, Baron Marcellin de. *Mémoires.* 3 vols. (Paris, 1891).

Marshall-Cornwall, Sir James. *Marshal Masséna* (London, 1965).

Martinien, Aristide. *Tableaux par corps et par batailles des Officiers tués et blessés pendant les guerres de l'Empire, 1805-1815* (Paris, 1899).

Parquin, Denis Charles. *Napoleon's Army.* Translated and edited by B. T. Jones (London, 1969).

Rigondaud, A. (Rigo). *Le Plumet* (Uniform plates). (Paris, n.d.).

Rousset, Camille (ed.). *Recollections of Marshal Macdonald, Duke of Tarentum.* Translated by Stephen Louis Simeon. Revised edition (London, 1893).

Ségur, Count Philippe Paul de. *History of the Expedition to Russia, undertaken by the Emperor Napoleon in the year 1812.* 2 vols. (London, 1825).

Six, Georges. *Dictionnaire biographique des généraux et amiraux français de la Révolution et de l'Empire.* 2 vols. (Paris, 1934).

Sloane, William Milligan. *The Life of Napoleon Bonaparte.* 4 vols. (New York/London, 1896).

Weller, Jac. *Wellington in the Peninsula, 1808-1814* (London, 1962).